THE SCOTTISH REGENCY
OF THE EARL OF ARRAN

A Study in the Failure of Anglo-Scottish Relations

James Hamilton, Second Earl of Arran and Governor of Scotland
In the Hamilton Collection, Scotland
Artist Unknown

THE SCOTTISH REGENCY
OF THE EARL OF ARRAN

A Study in the Failure of Anglo-Scottish Relations

David Franklin

Studies in British History
Volume 35

The Edwin Mellen Press
Lewiston/Queenston/Lampeter

Library of Congress Cataloging-in-Publication Data

Franklin, David Byrd.
    The Scottish regency of the Earl of Arran : a study in the failure
of Anglo-Scottish relations / David Franklin.
        p.   cm. -- (Studies in British history ; v. 35)
    Originally presented as the author's thesis (Ph. D.--University of
Alabama, 1981).
    Includes bibliographical references and index.
    ISBN 0-7734-8971-1 (hc)
    1. Scotland--History--Mary Stuart, 1542-1567. 2. Arran, James
Hamilton, Earl of, d. 1575. 3. Scotland--Politics and
government--16th century. 4. England--Foreign relations--Scotland.
5. Scotland--Foreign relations--England. 6. Regency--Scotland.
I. Title. II. Series.
DA786.F73 1995
941.105'092--dc20
[B]   94-41356
                                                                 CIP

This is volume 35 in the continuing series
Studies in British History
Volume 35 ISBN 0-7734-8971-1
SBH Series ISBN 0-88946-450-2

A CIP catalog record for this book is available from the British Library.

The Edwin Mellen Press   The Edwin Mellen Press
        Box 450   Box 67
Lewiston, New York   Queenston, Ontario
USA 14092-0450   CANADA L0S 1L0

The Edwin Mellen Press, Ltd.
Lampeter, Dyfed, Wales
UNITED KINGDOM SA48 7DY

Printed in the United States of America

To Louisa

TABLE OF CONTENTS

PREFACE AND ACKNOWLEDGMENTS

Flaws in the personality of political leadership seldom work to the advancement of national interest. An exception to this is James Hamilton, the second earl of Arran and governor of Scotland during the minority of Mary Queen of Scots. Arran's temperament--usually described as inconstant and vacillating in the extreme--combined with his inexperience in politics convinced the English, notably Henry VIII, that he would be the perfect catspaw whereby Scotland could be subjugated to England. Little did the English know that Arran had gained control of a government where the giant Henry was to be constantly deceived by little men. This book is the story of one such deceit--the earl of Arran's.

I would like to thank a few of the people who contributed in various ways to the completion of this book. Professors Bernerd C. Weber and Robert E. Johnson, both of the University of Alabama, gave excellent advice in the research and writing of the original draft. The staff at the British Library was very helpful, particularly in microfilming of pertinent manuscripts in its collection. Dean Clay Dotson of Young Harris College offered inspiration and incentive to complete the task of publication. Dean Glen Eaves of Mississippi College gave helpful suggestions toward the end of the process. To all of them, I am very indebted.

Most importantly, however, I thank my family. First, my parents, "Dot" and "Ug" Franklin, who provided meaningful education that made this work possible. Second, my children, Meg and John, who brought delight during moments of frustration in working. Third, my wife, Louisa, mostly for just being herself--who could ask for more?

David Franklin

Young Harris, Georgia

All dates in this study are new style

INTRODUCTION

The relationship between England and Scotland from the late thirteenth century until the mid-sixteenth century was particularly difficult. In 1286, the Scottish King Alexander III died, precipitating a major constitutional crisis in his kingdom. His successor, an infant granddaughter, Margaret, the "Maid of Norway," also died some four years later on her voyage from Norway to Scotland. A dispute concerning the succession to the Scottish throne soon arose. Thirteen claimants of the crown emerged--the two most important being Robert Bruce and John Balliol. Faction-ridden Scotland found it difficult to resolve this crisis alone. Therefore, Edward I of England was called upon to arbitrate between the claimants and to judge their various assertions.

The English king was a logical choice as arbiter because the Scottish guardians, or regents, had earlier agreed to their young queen's marriage to Edward's heir provided that Scotland's sovereignty would be maintained. The chief contenders, however, realizing that their fate lay with Edward's verdict, acknowledged his claim of overlordship in Scotland. Finally, during 1292, in the Award of Norham, the English monarch ruled in favor of Balliol.

Notwithstanding the apparent guarantee of Scottish sovereignty, Edward's insistence that Scottish legal cases be appealed to English courts and that the Scottish king should perform military service for him in France, indicated that Scotland was to be subordinated to England.

Sensing the blatant and bold English designs upon Scotland, Balliol in 1295 formed what has come to be known as "the auld alliance" with England's continental enemy, France. This alliance was to play a profound role in directing Scottish foreign policy until the mid-sixteenth century.

Edward, determined to rectify this disadvantageous situation, invaded Scotland during the following year. When he deposed Balliol and proclaimed himself the new king of the northern kingdom, a strong sense of Scottish nationalism was kindled--the Scottish war for independence had begun in earnest.

Following the death of Edward I in 1307, the Scots began to capitalize upon the weaknesses of the new English king, Edward II. The leader of the Scottish independence movement, Robert Bruce the Younger, scored a tremendous military victory at Bannockburn in 1314.

Fourteen years later a formal peace was established between the two British kingdoms. The treaty of Northampton acknowledged Bruce as king of Scotland, and English claims upon Scottish sovereignty were renounced. To insure the sincerity of this perpetual peace, the son of Robert Bruce was to marry the sister of the new English king, Edward III.

Unfortunately, perpetual peace between the English and the Scots was most difficult to achieve, marriage or no marriage. Hostilities--ranging from outright invasions to border raids--between the two neighbors continued on through the fourteenth and fifteenth centuries until the year 1502 when a new perpetual peace was concluded. Once again a dynastic marriage between Margaret Tudor, the daughter of the English king, Henry VII, and the Scottish king himself, James IV, was to show the sincerity of the former enemies in settling their differences once and for all. Regrettably, this perpetual peace lasted only until the eve of the battle of Flodden, for the aggressive foreign policy of Henry VIII forged a renewal of "the auld alliance" in 1512 which led to this Scottish disaster one year later. James IV lay dead on the battlefield along with representatives of virtually every significant Scottish family.[1]

The long minority of James' son and successor, James V, witnessed a struggle between two factions--those who championed "the auld alliance" and those who catered to the English in an effort to avoid another such disaster. When James began his personal rule in 1528, he clearly began to drift towards France. During the 1530's he found two wives in that kingdom. The first was Madeleine of Valois who died in 1537, less than a year after their marriage. Then in 1538, James wed the twenty-two year old wealthy widow Mary of Guise-Lorraine; their daughter succeeded him as Mary Queen of Scots.

The policies of James, both foreign and domestic, failed to win him much popularity either at home or abroad. Chief among his enemies was his Protestant uncle, Henry VIII, who persistently urged James to follow his direction in religious concerns to no avail. In 1541, the English king decided

---

[1]A rich collection of seldom used sources is Henry Ellis, ed., *Original Letters, Illustrative of English History; Including Numerous Royal Letters: From Autographs in the British Museum, and One or Two Other Collections. With Notes and Illustrations*, first series, 3 vols. 2nd ed. (London: Harding, Triphook, and Lepard, 1825), second series, 4 vols. (London: Harding and Lepard, 1827), third series, 4 vols. (London: Richard Bentley, 1846). Particularly significant are: third series, 1:33-39, "Letter presenting a Journal of Edward the Third's last expedition against the Scots, A.D. 1336," 3 August 1336, pp. 109-111, "James the Third of Scotland to King Richard the Third, desiring a safe-conduct for certain Lords of his realm to come in embassy to conclude a Peace," 6 November ?, pp. 111-3, "King Richard the Third's answer to the King of Scots concerning the safe-conduct which he granted; but staying the Abstinence from War desired in the same Letter, till the arrival of the Scots Embassy," 2 December ?, pp. 163-4, "Another Account of the Battle of Floddon, A.D. 1513, in a Letter from Dr. William Knight, the English Minister at the Court of Margaret Duchess of Burgundy, to Cardinal Bainbridge at Rome," 20 September 1513, and first series, 1:76-78, "King James the Fourth to King Henry the Eighth," 24 May 1513. (Hereafter cited as Ellis, *Original Letters*.) Two excellent accounts used in this introductory survey of Anglo-Scottish relations are John D. Mackie's "Henry VIII and Scotland," *Transactions of the Royal Historical Society*, fourth series, no. 29 (London: Offices of the Royal Historical Society, 1947), pp. 93-114, (hereafter cited as Mackie, "Scotland"), and William Ferguson's *Scotland's Relations with England: A Survey to 1707* (Edinburgh: John Donald Publishers Ltd., 1977), (hereafter cited as Ferguson, *Relations*).

that his backdoor, now recovered from the aftermath of Flodden, must be secured. Resolved to force the northern kingdom into acquiescence, Henry progressed northward to York in an effort to meet and overawe his nephew, the Scottish king. The Scottish council, however, fearful that its sovereign might be kidnapped, refused to let James enter England. Having waited in vain, the impatient Henry vowed to seek revenge.[2]

The English king by early 1542 had come to an agreement with the Holy Roman Emperor, Charles V, which committed the two to an invasion of France. Henry's backdoor, however, was still not secure. In an effort to provoke the Scots into open warfare, the English king ordered the duke of Norfolk in October to invade Scotland. Countering this blow, James V mustered an army which was thoroughly routed in November by the English at Solway Moss, one of the worst catastrophes in early modern Scottish history.

Even though Solway Moss had temporarily secured Henry's northern frontier, his commitment to the emperor and the continental war was halfhearted. The defeat of the Scots had opened up a new possibility for ending the unpleasant history of Anglo-Scottish relations, and the fifty-one year old Henry,

---

[2]Anglo-Scottish relations during the reign of James V are thoroughly covered by Richard Glen Eaves in his two works, *Henry VIII's Scottish Diplomacy, 1513-1524; England's Relations with the Regency of James V* (New York: Exposition Press, 1971) and *Henry VIII and James V's Regency, 1524-1528: A Study in Anglo-Scottish Diplomacy* (Lanham, Maryland: University Press of America, 1987). A survey of the reigns of Henry VIII, Edward VI, and Mary I is G. R. Elton's *Reform and Reformation: England, 1509-1558* (Cambridge, Massachusetts: Harvard University Press, 1977), pp. 305-6. (Hereafter cited as Elton, *Reform and Reformation*.) Two pertinent letters found in Ellis, *Original Letters*, second series, 1:289-91 are "Sir Thomas More to Cardinal Wolsey, upon the Affairs of Scotland," 21 September ? and third series, 2:303-6, "Andrew Boorde to Cromwell, from Glasgow, where he was studying Physic. His opinion of the Scots," 1 April ?.

now in declining health, was determined to pursue it.[3] Having revived the claim of Edward I when he declared war upon the Scots in 1542, Henry VIII reasserted his suzerainty or "the title of the English kings to the supremacy of Scotland."[4] Solway Moss had seemingly confirmed the validity of that belief just as the immediate aftermath of this victory convinced Henry that he could easily accomplish his designs. He hoped that yet another perpetual peace and dynastic union would be the cover by which he might finally gain political control of his neighbor to the north.

---

[3]Elton, *Reform and Reformation*, pp. 305-6.

[4]*The Complaynt of Scotlande: Ane Exortatione to the Thre Estaits to Be Viligante in the Deffens of Their Public Veil. 1549. With an Appendix of Contemporary English Tracts; The Just Declaration of Henry VIII (1542); The Exhortacion of James Harrysone, Scottisheman (1547), the Epistle of the Lord Protector Somerset (1548). The Epitome of Nicholas Bodrugan alias Adams (1548). Reedited from the Originals with Introduction and Glossary by James A. H. Murray* (London: N. Trubner and Co., 1872), xv and 191-206. (Hereafter cited as *Complaynt of Scotlande*.)

CHAPTER I

The Establishment of the Arran Regency

Henry VIII, already elated over his devastating defeat of the Scots at Solway Moss on 24 November 1542, soon learned that James V had died on 14 December. Grief over his losses in battle had proved too great for the Scottish king to bear. Blood relation or not, the English king took additional satisfaction in this latest development. Now, his claim to suzerainty over Scotland seemed stronger than it had ever been. A six day old girl, Mary Queen of Scots, now separated the grasping king from the throne of his northern neighbor. As the intelligence reports on this rapid chain of events trickled in, Henry acted without delay in planning his strategy for the coming year in regard to his grandniece's kingdom.[1]

The council of Scotland first officially notified Henry of James' death on 21 December, but he had received the news earlier when English dispatches of

---

[1]Great Britain, General Registry Office of Births, Deaths, and Marriages, *The Hamilton Papers, Letters and Papers Illustrating the Political Relations of England and Scotland in the XVIth Century, Formerly in the Possession of the Dukes of Hamilton, Now in the British Museum,* ed. Joseph Bain, 2 vols. (Edinburgh: Her Majesty's General Register House, 1890), 1:328-51. (Hereafter cited as *Hamilton Papers.*)

17 December had reached him.[2]   Found enclosed with this English correspondence was a separate letter bearing information on the Scottish king shortly before his death.   James and his uncle had not always agreed on what was best for the British kingdoms, religious differences having been particularly annoying to both.   Nevertheless, out of fear of losing control of his whole kingdom, the Scottish king stated a strong desire to establish peace with his southern neighbor.   Death, however, had brought not only an end to James' dreams, but a significant alteration in the course of Anglo-Scottish relations as well.[3]

Instead of dealing with a chastised nephew, the English king suddenly found himself confronted with a hastily assembled Scottish regency council which would attempt to lead the nation during this trying period. Despite the death of their leader, Henry did not intend to show much clemency to the Scots' cause.[4]

The English aim, so greatly furthered by the success at Solway Moss, was not yet completely attained. A weakened but still independent Scotland stood as an obstacle to Henry's grandiose scheme--the destruction of his neighbor's sovereignty. His means of undermining Scotland were, however, to show a notable shift of emphasis as he moved away from the battlefield and

---

[2]Great Britain, Record Commission, *State Papers Published under the Authority of His Majesty's Commission: Henry VIII*, 11 vols. (London: His Majesty's Commission, 1836), 5:230-2, The council of Scotland to Henry 8, 21 December 1542. (Hereafter cited as *State Papers.*) *Hamilton Papers*, 1:336, Lisle to Henry 8, 17 December 1542.

[3]Ibid., p. 337, Douglas to Lisle, 16 December 1542.

[4] Ibid., pp. 346-47, The council of England to the council of Scotland, 29 December 1542.

toward diplomatic channels.

Henry's new strategy depended upon a number of Scottish nobles and knights taken prisoner at Solway Moss. These so-called assured Scots were committed to the furtherance of a scheme which would allow the English king to gain control of a reformed Scotland. Scottish strongholds had to be secured. Of greater significance, however, was their pledge to place the young queen as well as the pro-French David Cardinal Beaton in Henry's hands on English soil.[5]

Beaton was born around 1494. He was the nephew of James Beaton, archbishop of St. Andrews. At sixteen he began his study of civil and canon law at Orléans. Later, Beaton became Scotland's resident at the French court. Following a distinguished clerical career, he was created a cardinal in 1538. One year later, Beaton succeeded his uncle as the archbishop of St. Andrews. Beaton's political career began in 1529 when he became the Scottish lord privy seal. He was frequently sent on diplomatic missions such as those which resulted in James V's two French marriages. The cardinal was a loyal supporter of "the auld alliance" and was an ardent opponent of Henry VIII and the English.

Among Henry's Scottish agents were the leaders of the Douglas clan. The earl of Angus and his brother, Sir George, although not captives but English pensioners exiled from their native country, willingly entered into treasonous

---

[5]Thomson, Thomas, ed., *A Diurnal of Remarkable Occurrents that Have Passed Within the Country of Scotland Since the Death of King James the Fourth till the Year M.D. LXXV.* (Edinburgh: the Bannatyne Club, 1833) p. 25. (Hereafter cited as *Diurnal*); *State Papers*, 5:232-5; *Hamilton Papers*, 1:347, the council of England to the council of Scotland, 29 December 1542 and p. 363, Henry 8 to Lisle, 8 January 1543.

accords with the king.[6] Angus was also distinguished by the fact that he was a former brother-in-law of Henry, having married the mother of James V--Margaret Tudor--in 1514. Angus' marriage to the English king's sister, however, ended in divorce in 1527. Despite this, the earl remained a partisan of the English cause.

Henry's Scotsmen pledged their loyalty to the king and his commanders--vowing to oppose any of the king's enemies, particularly those who sought to preserve Scottish independence or to serve French interests. Contemporaries referred to these assured Scots as "sworn Inglishmen," "fals Scots," or "Scottis inglismen."[7]

In view of the situation in which he found himself, Henry had reason to be confident that his plan of diplomacy for establishing suzerainty over Scotland would proceed with little trouble. The English king's confidence, however, was premature as events of the following year were to prove.

Frequently chaotic and unclear communications which reached Henry from Scotland during December 1542 were indicative of the situation which actually existed there. Confusion surrounding the establishment of the regency for the infant queen suggested that the road ahead for Scotland would be quite rough. Intrigues in this instance served to solidify Henry's resolve that his plan

---

[6]Ibid., pp. 351-52, Lisle to the privy council, 1 January 1543 and pp. 375-76, Angus' pledge, January 1543. Margaret Sanderson's *Cardinal of Scotland, David Beaton, c 1494-1546* (Edinburgh: John Donald Publishers Ltd., 1986) is a definitive life.

[7]M. H. Merriman, "The Assured Scots: Scottish Collaborators with England during the Rough Wooing," *Scottish Historical Review*, 47 (1968): 12. (Hereafter cited as Merriman, "The Assured Scots.")

of subversion would easily succeed.[8]

The traditional view states that the jockeying for governmental control began in Falkland Palace as the king lay dying. Although James would die with the satisfaction of knowing that at least he had a successor, he was dismayed when he learned of her sex. John Knox, a historian as well as a religious reformer, attributed to him the statement, "The devil go with it! It will end as it began: it came from a woman; and it will end in a woman. . . ."[9] Robert Lindsay of Pitscottie, a historian of the period, gave another version of the same story:

> . . . be this the post came out of Lythtgow schawing to the king goode tydingis that the quene was deliuerit. The king inquyrit: 'wither it was man or woman.' The messenger said 'it was ane fair douchter.' The king ansuerit and said. 'Adew, fair weill, it come witht ane lase, it will pase witht ane lase,' and so he recomnendit himself to the marcie of Almightie god and spak ane lyttill then frome that tyme fourtht, bot turnit his bak into his lordis and his face into the wall.[10]

Into this dramatic setting entered the machinations of Beaton, who sought an

---

[8]*Hamilton Papers*, 1:348-50, Lisle, etc., to Henry 8, 30 December 1542.

[9]John Knox, *History of the Reformation in Scotland*, first published 1584, ed. William Croft Dickinson, 2 vols. (London: Thomas Nelson and Sons, 1949), 1:39. (Hereafter cited as Knox, *History*.)

[10]Robert Lindsay of Pitscottie, *The Historie and Chronicles of Scotland from the Slaúchter of King James the First to the Ane Thousande Fyve Hundreith Thrie Scoir Fyftein Zeit, Written and Collected by Robert Lindesay of Pitscottie Being a Continuation of the Translation of the Chronicles Written by Hector Boece, and Translated by John Bellenden. Now First Published from Two of the Oldest Manuscripts, One Bequeathed by Dr. David Laing to the University of Edinburgh, and the Other in the Library of John Scott of Halkshill, C.B.*, ed. Aeneas James George Mackay, 3 vols. (Edinburgh: William Blackwood and Sons, 1899). Printed for the Scottish Text Society, 1:407. (Hereafter cited as Pitscottie, *Historie*.)

answer from the dying king concerning the question of his daughter's minority. Although James' answer as well as the intrigues themselves are still far from certain, the cardinal did not enjoy more than transitory success by producing shortly after the king's death a will which named himself head of a regency council. Included on this council were the earls of Huntly, Argyle, and Moray.[11]

The existence or non-existence of this will has provided the basis for one of the great controversies in sixteenth-century Scottish history. According to most accounts of James' death, Beaton handed the dying king a blank sheet of paper and helped him sign his name. Thus, the cardinal was able to produce a spurious will of his own choosing--one which gave him a free hand in Scottish affairs.

Beaton had been on generally bad terms with the Scottish king since the rout at Solway Moss. The cardinal had encouraged James to respond to Norfolk's invasion even though support from a great part of the nobility was lacking. Hence, James blamed Beaton for this disaster.[12] It seems logical, therefore, that the cardinal might very well have acted in this fashion as he feared his exclusion from governmental power.

Beaton's will, however, has never been found. No one has claimed to have actually seen it. Beyond rumor and one questionable document, the only

---

[11]Knox, *History*, 1:41; Andrew Lang, "The Cardinal and the King's Will," *Scottish Historical Review*, 3 (1906):410-22. (Hereafter cited as Lang, "King's Will"; Great Britain, *Historical Manuscripts Commission, Eleventh Report, Appendix, Part VI. The Manuscripts of the Duke of Hamilton, K.T.* (London: Her Majesty's Stationery Office, 1887), pp. 219-20. (Hereafter cited as *Historical Manuscripts Commission, Eleventh Report.*)

[12]*Hamilton Papers*, 1:334, Eure to Lisle, 13 December 1542; Humphrey Drummond, *Our Man in Scotland; Sir Ralph Sadleir, 1507-1587*, (London: Leslie Frewin, 1969), p. 58.

extant evidence of it is found in a conversation which took place at Holyrood in April 1543 between the object of this study, James Hamilton, the second earl of Arran, who had by this time become governor, and the English ambassador, Sir Ralph Sadler. Arran described how the cardinal ". . . did counterfeit the late king's testament; and when the king was almost dead, he took his hand in his and so caused him to subscribe a blank paper."[13] In response, Henry, not quite two weeks later, instructed Sadler to ask the governor, ". . . can youe think that youe shall contynue a governour when thadverse partie that wold have made themselves by a forged will regentes with youe, or rather excluded youe, shall have auctoritie. . .?"[14] Whether or not a will motivated the following is uncertain, but in late December 1542, Arran said that he planned to expose whatever lies the cardinal had told the council in the king's name.[15] Beaton, it seemed, was quite adept at discerning the wishes of the dead king.

Relations between the future governor and the cardinal during this trying period were very difficult. Arran, for example, expressed his contempt for Beaton by referring to him as a "false churle" at whom he would have drawn his sword had not other members of the council been between them.[16]

Although specific reasons for this outburst of hostility are unknown, there

---

[13]Arthur Clifford, ed., *The State Papers and Letters of Sir Ralph Sadler, Knight Banneret. To Which Is Added a Memoir of the Life of Sir Ralph Sadler, with Historical Notes by Walter Scott, Esq.*, 2 vols. (Edinburgh: Archibald Constable and Co., 1809), 1:138, Sadler to Henry 8, 12 April 1543. (Hereafter cited as *Sadler's State Papers*); *Hamilton Papers*, 1:512, Sadler to Henry 8, 12 April 1543.

[14]Ibid., p. 527, Henry 8 to Sadler, 25 April 1543. See Appendix III.

[15]Ibid., p. 348, Lisle, etc., to Henry 8, 30 December 1542.

[16]Ibid., p. 349.

were rather obvious factors which strained the relationship between these men who were in fact cousins. Arran, as the second person in the realm, was Mary's successor should she fail to maintain the Stuart royal line. His claim to this royal succession came by way of James II's daughter, Mary, who had married James, Lord Hamilton. The marriage produced James Hamilton, the first earl of Arran, who took as his third wife, Janet Beaton--the cardinal's aunt. This third union produced the earl in question. Therefore, not Beaton, but the second earl of Arran, although only in his mid-twenties and politically inexperienced, held the best claim to leadership in the queen's government. Hence, if there were indeed substance to the will, as Arran later maintained, then he most definitely had been excluded by the cardinal from a position which was by right his.

The earl's importance in Scottish history prior to 1542 was apparently negligible. Although the details of his early life are unclear, it is known that he was raised by his natural half-brother, Sir James Hamilton of Finnart, while his father was abroad. In 1529, he inherited his earldom following his father's death. Around 1532, Arran married Lady Margaret Douglas, the eldest daughter of the third earl of Morton. In 1536, the young earl accompanied James V to France where the Scottish king was seeking a bride from that kingdom. Such inexperience probably served as sufficient cause in Beaton's estimation to try and keep Hamilton from exercising the powers which were inherent in his title.

Another factor which clearly worked against harmony between the two relatives was the fact that the earl leaned towards a type of Protestantism not much different from that found in the kingdom which had so thoroughly routed the Scots at Solway Moss.[17] On the other hand, as pointed out earlier, Beaton was pro-French and Catholic. Yet, despite Arran's claim, it is certain that the cardinal, regardless of reasons, managed to hold an upper hand in Scottish affairs during the final days of December 1542. In view of this rivalry, it is probable that almost four months later Arran deliberately lied to Sadler about the cardinal's will. Why, for example, if he had known of the existence of such a document, did he not make specific reference to it before April? Arran was not even present at the famous deathbed scene. Hence, the story of the forged will might have been formulated in the earl's imagination.[18]

The evidence indicates that even if such a will did exist, Arran was never completely excluded from power as John Knox would have one believe. True, there exists the famous notarial instrument of Henry Balfour which substantiates the appointment of a regency council which would have excluded him from the government.[19] Knox, however, does not appear to have ever seriously questioned the document's value. This is somewhat understandable because Balfour's instrument is the only extant document in this famous controversy which attempts to delineate the final wishes of James V.

At first glance, the document seems credible. A closer examination of events immediately following the king's death, however, brings its validity into question. Only three days after James' death the earl of Arran was associated with Beaton and the three other named regents. On 17 December, George Douglas reported that a number of great men in Scotland had convened in

---

[17]Additional 32,649 folio 80, Arran to Lisle, 18 January 1543.

[18]Lang, "King's Will," pp. 411 and 419-22.

[19]*Historical Manuscripts Commission, Eleventh Report*, pp. 219-20.

Edinburgh for the purpose of choosing four governors, namely the earls of Arran, Moray, Huntly, and Argyle. He also specified that Beaton was to be named governor of the young queen and the council's head.[20]

On 19 December, Viscount Lisle, the future duke of Northumberland, who had recently been appointed commissioner to Berwick and the borders of Scotland, wrote the king that Beaton and only three of the earls had taken upon themselves the queen's government. The missing earl in this instance was not Arran, but Argyle. Lisle went on to report the rumor that James had died of poison and was secretly buried.[21] Again, on 21 December, the viscount informed the English privy council that the dead king had actually willed that Arran--not named in the questionable notarial instrument--should be included in the government.[22] Hence, whatever the validity and purpose of Balfour's document, it proved unsuccessful in keeping Arran from taking a seat on Beaton's regency council which was officially proclaimed on 19 December.[23]

The cardinal's ascendancy, however, quickly began to wane. By the beginning of January, the laird of Grange had advised Arran as second person in the realm to call an assembly of the nobility to settle the complicated regency question. Judging from Knox's account, Beaton's faction was violently opposed to Arran heading the government. The cardinal made it a point to manipulate

---

[20]*Hamilton Papers*, 1:340, George Douglas to Lisle, 17 December 1542.

[21]Barrett L. Beer, *Northumberland: The Political Career of John Dudley, Earl of Warwick and Duke of Northumberland* (n.p.: Kent State University Press, 1973), pp. 13-14. (Hereafter cited as Beer, *Northumberland*); *Hamilton Papers*, 1:342, Lisle to Henry 8, 19 December 1542.

[22]Ibid., p. 345, Lisle, etc., to the privy council, 21 December 1542.

[23]Ibid., pp. 345-6, Lisle to Henry 8, 24 December 1542.

the sentiments of a nation all too easily given to clannish feuds as he condemned not so much the earl, but rather his family:

> . . . For who knows not (said the Cardinal), that the Hamiltons are cruel murderers, oppressors of innocents, proud, avaricious, double, and false; and finally, the pestilence in this commonwealth.[24]

Arran responded:

> . . . Defraud me not of my right, and call me what ye please. Whatsoever my friends have been, yet unto this day, has no man cause to complain upon me, neither yet am I minded to flatter any of my friends in their evil doing; but by God's grace shall be as forward to correct their enormities, as any within the realm can reasonably require of me. And therefore, yet again, my Lords, in God's name I crave that ye do me no wrong, nor defraud me not of my just title before that ye have experience of my government.[25]

From such passages, it is quite clear that Knox wrote in terms of saints and sinners, with the former triumphing as Arran was praised and declared sole governor. Knox recorded that as a result of this victory, the king's possessions, including his "Palace, treasure, jewels, garments, horse, and plate," were placed the governor's hands.[26]

The proclamation which declared Arran regent of Scotland during the

---

[24]Knox, *History*, 1:41.

[25]Ibid.

[26]Ibid., pp. 41-42; *Hamilton Papers*, 1:360, Lisle to the privy council, 5 January 1543. See George Buchanan's description in *The History of Scotland from the Earliest Accounts of that Nation to the Reign of King James VI*, ed. Mr. Bond, 2 vols. (London: S. Palmer, 1722), 2:183-6. (Hereafter cited as Buchanan, *History*.)

queen's minority, has been described as more apparent than real. Arran's victory was only made possible by a compromise with the powerful prelate. Sometime shortly before he was chosen governor, Arran received the notarial instrument from the cardinal in exchange for the earl's promise that he would give the archbishop of Glasgow's Great Seal to Beaton. Hence, the cardinal relinquished the best evidence he had supporting his claim to leadership in exchange for the position of chancellor.[27] Beaton did this in order to maintain just enough contact with the inexperienced governor so as to make him "wax in his hands." Thus, Arran's affinities towards Protestantism and English interests would be checked. In more precise terms, it was Beaton's intention to make the governor his puppet, thereby defeating the ambitions of the English king and preserving the independence of Scotland.[28]

In conclusion, the evidence associated with the aftermath of James V's death suggests that Scotland was caught in a most unexpected and disquieting position. As the consequences of their defeat at Solway Moss were just becoming evident, the Scots' main stabilizing force quickly passed away. James did, nevertheless, manage to bequeath his kingdom an infant heir--hardly the type of leader Scotland so desperately needed at this critical moment in its history. In short, recent events had made the Scots even more susceptible to the ominous designs of their southern neighbor.

Sensing this vulnerability, the strongest man in the realm immediately stepped forward to insure the safety of his nation. Beaton, regardless of the validity of the infamous forged will and Balfour's notarial instrument, took the

---

[27]Lang, "King's Will," p. 417.

[28]Ibid., p. 413.

queen's government into his own hands. The cardinal was never so naive as to believe that clan-ridden Scotland would readily accept his sole leadership. Hence, he formed a council composed of four of the mightiest nobles in the land--the earls of Huntly, Moray, Argyle, and most importantly, the earl of Arran. By heading such a council, Beaton hoped to enable his nation to put up as strong a front as was possible against Henry.

The cardinal, however, had overstepped his mark, for the young and inexperienced earl of Arran, as second person in the realm, was by right both Mary's protector and governor. In January, enough Scotsmen had acknowledged this claim to insure Arran's primacy in the government. Beaton, however, was not completely overshadowed by Arran's victory. His consolation, irrespective of the means of attaining it, was the Great Seal of the chancellorship.

Despite the many complexities and uncertainties of this intriguing period of Scottish history, within only three weeks of James V's death, the regency question of his daughter's reign was finally settled. Just as many Scots sought to strengthen their state by rallying behind Arran, Henry VIII was diligently at work outlining his new strategy intended to do the very opposite. A foundation had been laid during these crucial days upon which a new phase of Anglo-Scottish relations would be built. No one yet knew what an unfortunate chapter it would turn out to be.[29]

---

[29]Jenny Wormald's "Bloodfeud, Kindred, and Government in Early Modern Scotland" in *Past and Present* 87 (1980): 54-97 is quite useful for the period in general.

CHAPTER II

The Early Months of Power

The proclamation of Arran as protector and governor of Scotland during the minority of Mary Queen of Scots was not welcomed in London. Most of Scotland might consider their new leader the second person in the realm, but the English king thought otherwise. Not Arran, but Henry, should have possession of the young queen of Scotland whereby he could decide the fate of his northern neighbor as its lawful suzerain.[1] The apparent display of unity shown by a select group of the Scottish nobility in its choice of Arran also disturbed the English king. A regency council likely to fall into sharp divisions pleased Henry more than the rule of one man. Lisle, realizing the dangers inherent in Scottish unity, described for his king how he worked not only at making friends for Henry, but also at keeping the Scottish lords from agreeing as much as possible in an effort to prevent them from conspiring against English interests.[2] Seemingly, Arran's appointment was the first setback to the king's subversive scheme which appeared certain of success during the month of December.

---

[1]*Hamilton Papers*, 1:363, Henry 8 to Lisle, 8 January 1543.

[2]Ibid., p. 350, Lisle, etc. to Henry 8, 30 December 1542.

Henry's response to Arran's success was realistic as he acknowledged that his assured Scots might need more help than was envisioned when the scheme was formulated.[3] Control of the young governor or "the pretendid Protectour," as Henry later styled him, had now also become a major priority of the assured Scots' mission.[4]

Obviously the most important key to the success of the English enterprise was control of the infant Mary. She must be taken from her protector and securely placed in the king's own custody. Henry saw no better means of doing this than by having her joined in marriage to his young son, future Edward VI, for a dynastic union between the Tudor and Stuart lines would be the means of achieving a truly united Britain.[5] History had shown a certain validity to such hopes. Only time was needed to see them realized.

Although there was certainly very little evidence of it by 1543, a dynastic marriage had already created the nucleus from which a voluntary political union would be erected. Credit for solving this so-called British problem, however, belongs not to Henry but to his father, Henry VII. The success of the first Tudor's skillful diplomacy with the northern kingdom resulting in the marriage of James IV and Margaret Tudor--known as "the union of the thistle and the rose"--stood in stark contrast with Henry VIII's attempts to have Edward wed the young queen of Scots--popularly known as "the rough wooing."

There were problems in Henry's wooing. Prince Edward was not the

---

[3]Ibid., p. 363, Henry 8 to Lisle, 8 January 1543.

[4]Ibid., pp. 371 and 373, Henry's second instructions to Southwell, January 1543.

[5]*Diurnal*, p. 26; *Hamilton Papers*, 1:354-5, Henry 8 to the council of Scotland, 4 January 1543 and p. 374, Henry's second instructions to Southwell, January 1543.

only suitor of the young Stuart queen. A prime contender for her hand was the governor's own son.[6] Some suspected that Cardinal Beaton for his own nationalistic reasons favored this union of the Stuart and Hamilton houses.[7] Actually, Arran's son seemed the most advantageous choice for the Scots since there would be no question concerning the queen's residence after her marriage. On the other hand, if Mary were to wed the heir of another kingdom, she would be expected to reside in that country with her husband. A marriage of this kind would probably subsume the queen's realm to that of her husband.[8] Such, in fact, was Henry's intention.[9]

Initial English intelligence reports for January indicated little sentiment within Scotland favoring a match with Henry's young son. Betrothing her to a younger or second son of either the king of France or Denmark seemed a more logical possibility. Unfortunately for Henry, there was simply no second son available in England. This situation troubled the English king, who had already gone to extremes to produce the one legitimate male heir he did have. Scottish logic did seem sound, for the young man would become king of Scotland and dwell within his wife's kingdom.[10]

An obvious flaw, however, existed in the Scots' thinking which was

---

[6]Ibid., p. 358, Lisle and Tunstall to Henry 8, 5 January 1543.

[7]Ibid., p. 352, Lisle to the privy council, 1 January 1543; T. F. Henderson, *Mary Queen of Scots: Her Environment and Tragedy: A Biography*, 2 vols. (London: Hutchinson and Co., 1905), 1:44. (Hereafter cited as Henderson, *Mary Queen of Scots.*)

[8]*Hamilton Papers*, 1:358, Lisle and Tunstall to Henry 8, January 1543.

[9]Ibid., p. 374, Henry's second instructions to Southwell, January 1542 [sic].

[10]Ibid., p. 358, Lisle and Tunstall to Henry 8, 5 January 1543.

immediately recognized by the pro-English faction. Henry's longstanding rival on the continent, Francis I, had a second son--but he was a grown man with apparently little desire for joining a "suckling childe" in holy matrimony. The English prince, on the other hand, was of a convenient age.[11]

Convenient age or not, this was no reason for the Scots to change their attitude on the prospects of such a marriage, despite the implications of later intelligence reports. Fear of England played a large role in driving many Scots to choose Arran as their governor and head of the regency. That same fear would prevent this dynastic union from being realized, for many recognized that should a marriage between Prince Edward and Queen Mary take place, ". . . both the realmes shuld be as one, and Skotland clearly undone."[12] Lisle reported the reasoning behind this Scottish fear to Henry:

> . . . the realme of Skotland is but a pore thing to Englond, yet having the state of a kynge in yt self, all the revenues thereof shuld be spent within the realme, whereas if bothe the realmes were under one, all shuld go to the kinge of England out of the country of Skotland not to be spent their, whereby Skotland nowe being poore alredy, shulde be utterly beggered and undone, whiche . . . was the mynde of Skotland, whiche do desire to have a kinge amonges theym selves for their owne wealthe as they have alweys had.[13]

The major goal of Arran's regency was the preservation of Scottish independence. As the reins of state passed into his hands, he was plagued by

---

[11]Ibid.

[12]Ibid.

[13]Ibid.

thoughts similar to those entertained by James V shortly before his death. The new governor recognized Scotland's vulnerability and knew that the establishment of peace with the English king was of the utmost importance to the survival of his own government.

Since the Scots' rout at Solway Moss, Henry had held the upper hand in matters relating to the two kingdoms. Perhaps a belligerent English policy towards the Scots could frighten them into a marriage agreement which would serve as the basis of a lasting peace.[14] Henry's subversive activity would thereby be honorably disguised. On 29 December, the king's government placed the blame for the outbreak of war on its neighbor; complained that certain prisoners taken in battle by the Scots at Haddon Rig in August had not been returned; and stated that those who had "detestablye" murdered the English herald, Somerset, had also not been returned to their native land for the just punishment which awaited them.[15]

The Scots did not need Henry to remind them of these transgressions. As early as 21 December, the Scottish council had reported to the English government that the herald's murderers had been imprisoned by their late king and would be given up as desired by Henry.[16] By the end of December, Lisle reported that these murderers were to be delivered to the English at Berwick on

[14] A. J. Slavin, *Politics and Profit: A Study of Sir Ralph Sadler, 1507-1547* (Cambridge: Cambridge University Press, 1966), p. 102. (Hereafter cited as Slavin, *Politics and Profit*); *Hamilton Papers*, 1:354-5, Henry 8 to the council of Scotland, 4 January 1543; *State Papers*, 5:240-1, Lisle to Henry 8, 9 January 1543.

[15] *Hamilton Papers*, 1:346-7, the council of England to the council of Scotland, 29 December 1542. For a description of the herald's murder see *State Papers*, 5:225-7, Ray's narrative of the murder of Somerset Herald, December 1542.

[16] Ibid., pp. 230-2, the council of Scotland to Henry 8, 21 December 1542.

7 January.[17] Arran did all he could to satisfy Henry's demands on this subject, for the Scots were anxious to oblige the English king.[18] A communiqué of 21 December to the English council requested from Henry a safe-conduct for Scottish ambassadors and a five to six month armistice.[19] On 4 January, however, the English king evaded these requests and instead warned the Scottish government to come to terms with his demands without delay. These demands would be those made by his assured Scots upon returning home. If Arran's government should refuse to come to certain and plain terms with them, then Henry would not ". . . pretermit thopportunitie offered by God to unite thiese two realmes in oon governe[ment]."[20]

In spite of such evasions and bold talk, the Scots desperately pursued an armistice with the English. Arran, in his first letter to Henry as governor, repeated the request for a truce and safe-conduct which would enable his ambassadors to cross over into England for the purpose of achieving peace between the two kingdoms. The new governor also maintained that there was none more desirous of peace than his government. Hence, the Scots would do their utmost to procure it.[21] The reason behind this quest for peace is clear. The Scots had no alternate course to follow in view of the military supremacy of their rival. On 18 January, Arran reiterated these requests to Lisle, displaying

---

[17] *Hamilton Papers*, 1:351, Lisle, etc. to Henry 8, 30 December 1542; *State Papers*, 5:235-9, Lisle and Tunstall to Henry 8, 9 January 1543.

[18] Additional 32,649 folio 12, Arran to Lisle, 4 January 1543.

[19] *State Papers*, 5:230-2, the council of Scotland to Henry 8, 21 December 1542.

[20] *Hamilton Papers*, 1:354, Henry 8 to the council of Scotland 4 January 1543.

[21] Additional 32, 649, folios 22-23, Arran to Henry 8, 6 January 1543.

along with them an obvious proclivity towards religious reform:

> It has plesit God to call ws to the government of this
> realme, induring the tendir and les aige of our soverane Ladie
> (quhame God preserve), and we ar myndit with the grace and
> help of God, to put sum reformatioun in the stait of kirk of this
> realme to the hie honour of God, furtht setting of his trewe
> worde, and proffeit to our commone weil, the quhilk may nocht
> weil be done without gret inconvenient, weir standing betuix the
> twa realmis, as it dois instantlye; and gif your soverane and
> master be of mynde that Goddis worde accress and prosper in this
> realme, as we trast he is, we demit nocht bot his majeste wyll put
> away the cause and occatioun that is obstakle or impediment
> theirto; praying you heirfor rycht effectuously that ye wyll be the
> instrument, to addres ane salf conduct to be send fra your
> soverane to certane ambassatouris quhhilkis we purpois to send
> towart his majestie for contracting of the paice betuix the realmis
> to the honour of God, furtht setting of his Holy Worde, rest and
> tranquillitie of the inhabitants and faithfull subjects of athir of the
> realmis. . .[22]

Scottish and English priorities were diametrically opposed to one another:
the Scots seeking to preserve their independence from Henry's grasp; the
English wanting to subvert that independence by a policy of diplomatic deceit.
Peace between the two kingdoms, however, was necessary for either plan to
succeed. The subversive activities of Henry's assured prisoners would be
carried out much more effectively in conditions of peace than in those of war.
In fact, Lisle held the opinion that a safe-conduct and an armistice would

---

[22]*Hamilton Papers*, p. 383, the governor of Scotland to Lisle, 18 January 1543. Other
illustrations of the governor's desire for peace can be found in the *Hamilton Papers*, 1:401-2,
the governor to Suffolk; Additional 32,649 folio 108 for Suffolk's acknowledgement, 3 February
1543; Additional 32,649 folio 111, Arran to Lisle, 3 February 1543; and Additional 32,649 folio
117, again to Lisle, 5 February 1543.

actually tend to accentuate the already prevalent divisions within faction-ridden Scotland, hence working to his nation's advantage.[23] Henry, too, realized that peace was imperative, coming to the conclusion that he would have to win the leader of the Hamilton family wholeheartedly to his side if his plans were to progress smoothly. Even though the king continued to play a guessing game with his northern neighbor for a few days, his granting of a truce followed soon after his realization that Arran would be an easy person for his assured Scots to manipulate.

The proclamation of Arran as governor and head of the regency truly indicated a unity within Scotland that was contrary to Henry's purpose. The king, nevertheless, entertained thoughts that this development was more apparent than real. Arran, just as Henry and many others believed, was "but a sobre man in goodes and wittes."[24] As such, the young governor would not be able to stand up to his rival, Cardinal Beaton.[25] Henry, therefore, seized upon the idea of capitalizing on the threat of Beaton to the new government in hopes of winning its governor to the English side. The young leader should be reminded that the cardinal, although his cousin, was definitely in the French camp which favored the claim to leadership of Mathew Stuart, the fourth earl of Lennox, over Arran's own.[26]

Like Arran's claim, that of the earl of Lennox rested on his descent from

---

[23]*Hamilton Papers*, 1:407, Lisle to Suffolk, 7 February 1543.

[24]Ibid., pp. 369-70, Henry's second instructions to Southwell, January 1543; *State Papers*, 5:240-1, Lisle to Henry 8, 9 January 1543.

[25]*Hamilton Papers*, 1:370, Henry's second instructions to Southwell, January 1543.

[26]Ibid., p. 372 and p. 367, Henry 8 to Lisle, 8 January 1543.

James II's daughter, Mary, and her husband, James, Lord Hamilton. Yet, it was through their daughter Elizabeth rather than through their son James, the first earl of Arran, that Lennox's line was drawn. Elizabeth had married Mathew Stuart, the second earl of Lennox. From this union came John Stuart, the third earl of Lennox, who sired Mathew Stuart, the fourth earl of Lennox and rival of the governor. Arran's paternal claim, however, held precedence over the maternal claim of Lennox--provided one condition was established. Was Arran a legitimate issue of his father? This question would play a fundamental role in influencing the direction of Arran's regency, and it should not be underemphasized in evaluating the man as future events will show.

As previously noted, James Hamilton, the first earl of Arran, had three wives. His first wife was Beatrix Drummond, by whom he produced a daughter, Margaret. His second wife was Elizabeth Home, whom he divorced in November 1504, on the grounds that her prior husband, Thomas Hay, was still alive when their marriage took place. Hay had travelled abroad and was erroneously reported as dead. Allegedly, he was found alive in June 1491, just over one year after the earl's second marriage.[27] This divorce, for mysterious reasons, was repeated on 11 March 1510. The estranged Elizabeth, who continued to refer to herself as Lady Hamilton, finally died in 1544 some twenty-eight years after the earl's marriage to Janet Beaton, mother of the governor. Lennox later disputed the first earl's divorce on the grounds that Elizabeth's first husband was indeed dead when this second union occurred. Hence, the governor's father, according to Lennox, had no grounds for a divorce. The exact circumstances surrounding this whole controversy are by no

---

[27]George Hamilton, *A History of the House of Hamilton* (Edinburgh: J. Skinner and Col, Ltd., 1933), p. 12. (Hereafter cited as Hamilton, *House of Hamilton*.)

means clear and were frequently commented upon by the governor's contemporaries. This uncertainty, however, is what Lennox clung to in supporting his claim to power following James V's death. If the first earl's divorce were invalid, the second earl was obviously a bastard with no legal right whatsoever to the Scottish succession.[28]

With such a substantial claim lodged against his government, compounded by French support for the claim, the governor found himself in a vulnerable position. The English king, realizing Arran's dilemma, extended his assistance to the Scottish leader. Henry's overture, however, was obviously motivated by greed rather than by an unselfish desire to help. In view of the governor's predicament, Henry, as early as 8 January, instructed his emissaries to make it clear to Arran that his salvation lay with the English king. Henry wanted Arran to believe that if he were to retain any political influence whatsoever, the regency's policies must respond to the king's beck and call. In short, Arran's cause must become Henry's, and if this were ever actually to occur, Scottish independence would be lost.[29]

Had English reasoning been correct, the governor's options were obvious. He could fall prey either to Henry and the English faction on the one side or to

---

[28]Ibid.; Found in the Cotton manuscript collection, Caligula B VIII folios 198 and 218 are interesting notes concerning Arran and Lennox, as well as arguments and answers pertaining to the question of the governor's alleged illegitimacy; *Hamilton Papers*, 1:336, Lisle and Tunstall to Henry 8, 17 December 1542; Knox, *History*, 1:49; *Historical Manuscripts Commission, Eleventh Report*, pp. 49-51; *Dictionary of National Biography from the Earliest Times to 1900*, 2nd ed., s.v. "Hamilton, James, First Earl of Arran," by Thomas Finlayson Henderson. (Hereafter cited as *Dictionary of National Biography*.)

[29]*Hamilton Papers*, 1:367, Henry 8 to Lisle, 8 January 1543 and p. 372, Henry's second instructions to Southwell, January 1543; *State Papers*, 5:240-41, Lisle to Henry 8, 9 January 1543.

Beaton and the French camp on the other. Perhaps, however, Arran could avoid both extremes and prove this argument false.

Much pressure was brought to bear upon the governor to win him over to Henry. Accentuating the earl's predicament were rumors circulated by the English that the French duke of Guise was coming to Scotland to gain control of his young granddaughter, the queen. Reportedly, Guise was also intent upon taking Arran's government into his own hands. This French mission would be accomplished by the assistance of the cardinal, who still held the powerful office of chancellor in his rival's government.[30] Beaton, however, did not retain his office for long after the arrival of the assured Scots and the leaders of the Douglas family.

Rivalry similar in nature to that between Arran and Lennox ran rampant in sixteenth-century Scotland. The Hamiltons were at odds with the Lennox Stuarts, and with other families as well. Their greatest rivals in the past had been the Douglases, at that time led by the earl of Angus and his younger brother, Sir George, who as already indicated, were English pensioners playing prominent roles in Henry's attempt to gain political control of Scotland. The rivalry between these traditional enemies at first appeared to work against the success of the English king's mission. For example, one might suppose that Arran would be violently opposed to the Douglas brothers' return to their native land. On the other hand, just the opposite occurred as he enthusiastically

---

[30]*Hamilton Papers*, 1:385, the privy council to Lisle and Sir Francis Brian, 19 January 1543. On 12 February, Suffolk warned Arran of Guise's approach, Additional 32,649 folio 143. On 14 February, Arran wrote to Henry thanking him for his warning of Guise's plans, *Hamilton Papers*, 1:424-25. In Lisle to Suffolk's correspondence on 6 February, however, the governor appears to have been little troubled by the news of the approach of his enemy, the duke of Guise, ibid., p. 404. Arran and Angus gave little credence to this English report. Such skepticism was warranted in view of his failure to arrive as anticipated by the English.

greeted the younger Douglas upon his arrival in Edinburgh.[31] The cardinal, however, displayed skepticism as he received Sir George. The Scottish council, on which the Douglases regained their seats, was not oblivious to the assured Scots' mission, although Henry's basic intent was not yet known.[32] Beaton, perceiving the king's ultimate goal and disappointed that Douglas and Arran were not at each other's throats, attempted to disrupt their amity. Sensing a decline in his own power and the success of the pro-English Douglases, the cardinal acted out of desperation by reminding Arran of the traditional enmity which existed between these two families:

> . . . he went straight to therle of Arren, and did what he wolde to
> putt hym in a jelosie of therle of Anguishe and of hym, rehersing
> thole grudges, and putt hym in remembrance of the deithe of his
> kynesfolkes whiche therle of Anguishe did kyll, and bade hym
> take good heede of hymself, for they wolde do hym a shrwede
> turne if yt laye in their power.[33]

In response to this warning by the cardinal, Arran later declared to Sir George that Beaton ". . . was the falsest karle in the world." In addition, the governor stated that the cardinal had many times urged him to divorce his wife, herself a Douglas, in order to marry the queen dowager, Mary of Guise.[34] After degrading "this hollye father," Arran fully agreed with Sir George that as soon as Angus should return to Scotland, he would seize Beaton and send him

---

[31]Ibid, pp. 387-89, Lisle to Henry 8, 21 January 1543.

[32]Ibid., p. 390.

[33]Ibid., p. 389.

[34]Ibid.

to Henry if it were the king's desire to have him.[35] Such an attitude on the part of the governor who was not only given to peace, but who also stated his eagerness to meet Henry in person, delighted the English and gave a great deal of encouragement to their plans.[36] After all, possession of the cardinal was a major objective of the assured Scots' scheme. Arran's desire to reform the church in Scotland along Henrician lines also served as a powerful incentive for the capture of Beaton and his delivery to the English. A condition, however, had been placed by the governor upon such action--he must know that "sure quyetnes" existed between the two realms.[37]

Indications such as these made it seem that Arran would be easy for the English to manipulate. This optimistic view betrayed the inadequacy of English intelligence in fathoming the major developments and personalities in Scotland at that time. Lisle, for example, in late January seemed to have doubts about his own efficiency and suitability as one of Henry's informers. Failure to understand what motivated the Scots, particularly Arran, was a significant factor in the final collapse of Henry's mission that at times seemed so sure of success. The governor's desire to reform the Scottish church along English lines, for example, was interpreted by the English to mean that Arran would be a very faithful apostle of Henry's political designs as well. Although Lisle appeared to question his own observations and opinions more than most English emissaries, he sensed this overly optimistic spirit. While loyal to Henry's scheme of diplomacy at the Scottish court, Lisle saw much better than did the

---

[35]Ibid.

[36]Ibid. and p. 391.

[37]Ibid., p. 401, Douglas to Lisle, 26 January 1543.

king the political limitations of such a policy not adequately supported by military force.[38]

Nevertheless, reports to Henry described his agent, Sir George, as ". . . like to bere the grettist stroke with the said Erle of Arren of any man in Skotland."[39] In fact, the governor even offered Douglas his sister-in-law, the daughter of the earl of Morton, in marriage for his son who would also be made an earl.[40] Regardless of the governor's true priorities, such behavior as this probably dampened any earlier suspicions which Henry had concerning him. The possibility of problems caused by his initial proclamation as governor and head of the regency had lessened. By the end of January Arran seemed to be one of the king's own men, or at least nearly one of them.

On 27 January the agreement made to seize the cardinal was carried out.[41] He was taken at Holyrood Palace in the governor's chamber while meeting with the council. The queen dowager, inside the palace, was frightened by the disturbance to the extent of letting out "a great schryche." Angus pacified her, assuring her the fear she had that ". . . the lordes had byn togyders by the eares" was not true. The cardinal was imprisoned in Dalkeith, a Douglas fortress, about four miles outside of Edinburgh. Lisle, in reporting the seizure

---

[38]Beer, *Northumberland,* pp. 16-18; *Hamilton Papers,* 1:393-94, Lisle to the privy council, 22 January 1543 and p. 400, Lisle to Suffolk, 28 January 1543; *State Papers,* 5:240-41, Lisle to Henry 8, 9 January 1543.

[39]*Hamilton Papers,* 1:391, Lisle to Henry 8, 21 January 1543 and p. 398, Lisle to Suffolk, 28 January 1543.

[40]Ibid., p. 394, Lisle to the privy council, 22 January 1543.

[41]*Diurnal,* p. 26; *Hamilton Papers,* 1:397-98, Lisle to Suffolk, 28 January 1543; *State Papers,* 5:249, Lisle to Suffolk, 1 February 1543.

to Suffolk, held the opinion that rumors concerning the approach of the duke of Guise from France hastened the governor's action.[42] But Arran, for whatever reasons, had unwittingly advanced a major part of Henry's scheme for subverting Scottish independence. For the time being, Beaton was in relative safekeeping for the English.

Many Scots, however, were upset with the prelate's imprisonment. Lisle reported that there was not a priest within Scotland who would perform mass, christen, or bury since the cardinal's capture.[43] The governor also suffered a loss of popularity among some of "the ignorant and comen people" who resented the imprisonment of his foe as well as his close association with the Douglases.[44] Despite this, Lisle believed that Arran was too zealous in his preoccupation with church matters and was not enough concerned with the pursuance of Henry's political purpose.[45]

Despite the resentment of the masses, by early February Arran's prestige as regent of Scotland had increased with the ruling elite. A warmer relationship was established between the English and Scottish realms than had existed in early January. A safe-conduct for Scottish ambassadors to arrange a peace treaty with England was granted by a now more cooperative Henry.[46] An additional concession of the king to Arran was the naming of a qualified English

---

[42]*Hamilton Papers*, 1:397-98, Lisle to Suffolk, 28 January 1543.

[43]*State Papers*, 5:249, Lisle to Suffolk, 1 February 1543.

[44]*Hamilton Papers*, 1:426-27, Lisle to Suffolk, 15 February 1543.

[45]Ibid., p. 400, 28 January 1543.

[46]Additional 32,649 folio 119, Henry 8 to Arran, 9 February 1543.

agent, unlike his assured Scots, who would discuss with the governor the complicated problems which existed between the two kingdoms.[47]

To fulfill this request, Sir Ralph Sadler, a well-versed and experienced English envoy, who had first represented Henry in 1537 at the Scottish court, would shortly leave for Edinburgh.[48] Sadler was now in his mid-thirties and his familiarity with Scottish affairs had begun when he was sent to the northern kingdom to investigate the complaints against the Scots of the king's sister, the dowager Queen Margaret. He had also represented Henry in France where he was sent on an intelligence mission to discover the exact nature of "the auld alliance." Having distinguished himself on the continent, in 1540 Sadler was once again sent to Scotland where he advised James V against Cardinal Beaton and urged the king to adopt a reformist religious posture. Following this assignment, he was named as one of Henry VIII's two principal secretaries of state. The year before he left England for his latest Scottish mission, Sadler was knighted.

By consenting to Arran's requests, the English king actually acknowledged the sovereignty of that nation which he thought was by right his. In addition, these concessions signified Henry's total commitment to follow a scheme of subverting Scottish independence by diplomacy rather than by force.[49]

Henry was aware of the problems faced by his predecessors in attempting

---

[47]Additional 32,649 folio 106, Arran to Suffolk, 30 January 1543.

[48]Additional 32,650 folio 27, Henry 8 to Arran, 13 March 1543; Slavin, *Politics and Profit*, p. 104.

[49]Ibid.; *Hamilton Papers* l:xli.

to deal with the Scots by force, even when they were experiencing the most difficult of times.[50] He undoubtedly thought of this as the developments of December 1542 reached him, and he began to formulate his scheme of subversion. A letter of 9 February to Arran, however, officially signalled his intent to pursue a policy of peaceful co-existence with the Scots, no matter what his basic purpose was.[51]

The governor's conduct in office during his first two months had given Henry enough confidence to follow through quickly with his plans. His attitude towards the young governor had changed considerably. Instead of being anxious to lay his hands on "the pretendit Protector," Henry now showed signs of goodwill as he addressed his "Right trusty and right welbiloved cousin."[52] Such change of attitude on the part of the English king was significant. Henry thought that it was even within his power to influence Arran's choice of ministers and suggested that the earl of Glencairn replace Beaton as chancellor.[53] Somewhat later, James Drummond was recommended as his secretary of state.[54] Both Glencairn and Drummond were considered trustworthy instruments of the king's will.

Arran received other suggestions. Henry wanted Beaton placed in his own personal possession. Dalkeith and the governor's watchful eye were no

---

[50]Ibid., l:xxxviii.

[51]Additional 32,649 folio 119, Henry 8 to Arran, 9 February 1543.

[52]Ibid.

[53]*Hamilton Papers*, 1:410, the privy council to Angus and his brother, 10 February 1543.

[54]Additional 32,650 folio 26, Henry 8 to Arran, 13 March 1543; and *Hamilton Papers*, 1:466-7, the instructions to Sir Ralph Sadler, 13 March 1543.

longer good enough for the king's purposes. Hence, Lisle urged Arran secretly to transfer the prelate to Berwick, by way of Angus' stronghold, Tantallon Castle. Such action, he told the governor, made much sense in view of possible French intervention to set the cardinal at liberty.[55] Following this advice, Lisle moved on to specific religious concerns, urging the governor to choose an educated reformer as commissary and possible successor to Beaton in the primatial see of St. Andrews.[56] Lisle, in spite of his earlier qualms, continued to encourage Arran's proclivities towards religious reform. A vernacular translation of the Bible, for example, would help many a Scot in perceiving the truth and avoiding sedition.[57] If no such Bibles were to be found in Scotland, Lisle offered English assistance in obtaining them or meeting any other request which the governor might make.[58]

In spite of Henry's eagerness to give advice, Arran was not as susceptible to English influence as the king believed. On 17 February, the governor wrote to Lisle thanking him for his recommendations but maintaining that Beaton was in safe-enough hands. As regards Lisle's offer to help in disseminating the gospel, Arran desired assistance.[59] This unwillingness on the part of the governor to adhere to all of Henry's wishes was an early but important indication that Arran would be more difficult to deal with than he sometimes

---

[55]Suffolk also warned Arran of this French threat in Additional 32,649 folio 143, 12 February 1543; Additional 32,649 folio 150, Lisle to Arran, 13 February 1543.

[56]Ibid.

[57]Ibid.

[58]Ibid.

[59]Additional 32,649 folio 160, Arran to Lisle, 17 February 1543.

gave the impression of being.

The governor could afford to be somewhat obstinate in view of the fact that it was on the same day, 17 February, that he acknowledged Henry's correspondence granting a three month land truce and a safe-conduct for his ambassadors who were to set forth without delay. Perhaps trying to appease the king, Arran notified Henry that he had summoned a parliament for 12 March to reduce the forfeitures of the pro-English Douglases and their friends. As such he asked for an extension of the Solway prisoners' furlough from Palm Sunday until Whitsunday, so that they might be participants at this important occasion.[60] Henry agreed to this request one week later.[61]

Arran's first parliament, however, achieved a great deal more than the restoration of the Douglas faction.[62] The Douglases and the Solway prisoners, just as the governor believed, were not fit agents for negotiation with the Scottish government. Neither were they very successful in furthering Henry's plans. The Douglases, in particular, had minds quite independent of the king.[63] Sadler was to discover some of these rather obvious and disturbing flaws in the king's scheme even before his arrival in Scotland. In short, by the end of March, there were indications that events were not proceeding as smoothly as Henry had envisioned them even as late as the closing days of February.

During his early months of power, Arran had conducted himself in a

---

[60]*Hamilton Papers*, 1:428-9, the governor to Henry 8, 17 February 1543; Additional 32,649 folio 172, Arran to Suffolk, 20 February 1543.

[61]*Hamilton Papers*, 1:439-40, Henry 8 to the governor, 24 February 1543.

[62]*Diurnal*, p. 27.

[63]*Sadler's State Papers*, 1:101-3, Henry 8 to Sadler, 30 March 1543.

manner which served his nation's interests well. Governing Scotland was no easy responsibility, for sixteenth-century Scottish politics was complicated business--complicated even for a monarch of Henry's stature to fathom. The English king, however, was oblivious to this fact.

CHAPTER III

To Secure His King's Designs:
Sir Ralph Sadler in Scotland

A spirit of optimism surrounded Henry VIII's Scottish policy in February 1543. An apparent about face had taken place in the Scots' attitudes concerning the marriage of Prince Edward and Queen Mary. Reports such as that of Lisle to Henry in early January expressing apprehension among the Scots concerning the proposed union had by the middle of the following month reversed themselves.[1] Not only the earl of Moray, a conservative protégé of Beaton and former colleague of Arran on the cardinal's regency council, but the queen dowager herself had given genuine indications of a desire to see such a marriage treaty implemented. Faction-ridden Scotland, so it seemed to the English, had united in support of English interests. The lesson of Solway Moss had apparently been learned well. Henry's decision to subvert the political independence of Scotland by diplomacy rather than by force had seemingly been the correct choice.

According to English intelligence, even the conservative Moray knew his nation's place in relation to its English neighbor. The earl had shown as great a willingness as any man to serve the English king. In fact, there was no man

---

[1]*Hamilton Papers*, 1:417, Suffolk, etc., to the privy council, 13 February 1543.

alive who would rather see the two kingdoms of England and Scotland united in one government than he--". . . sayeng if all were oone we shulde be strong ynoughe to plucke the Great Turke oute of his denne."[2] The possibility that a united Britain led even by Henry could stand up to Suleiman the Magnificent, whose conquests in eastern Europe had staggered the imaginations of all the Christian states, was remote indeed. Henry, no doubt, realized this. What he failed to comprehend, however, were the realities of the Scottish situation--Arran being a major cause for such misunderstanding.

Reports continued to make reference to the governor's reforming propensities and his apparent pandering to the English side. In fact, Arran had already furthered the Protestant cause within his kingdom to the point of alienating a sizeable segment of its population. Dissatisfaction with the imprisonment of Beaton was intense within the Scottish capital. With the exception of Arran's and Angus' chaplains there were no priests to perform mass. Thomas Gwilliam, at one time the prior of the Black Friars monastery in Inverness, and the Protestant monk, John Rough, preached in the Scottish countryside in Lothian, Fife, and Angus. Although they were hailed in Dundee, they met with little success in Edinburgh. Only the protection of the two earls prevented the congregation from attacking them as they preached daily in either the abbey at Holyrood or in St. Giles' Cathedral.[3]

Such eagerness on the part of Arran to advance a cause which he and the king both supported led Henry to believe that the young queen of Scots was

---

[2]Ibid.

[3]Ibid., p. 418 and p. 426, Lisle to Suffolk, 15 February 1543; Jasper Ridley, *John Knox*, (New York and Oxford: Oxford University Press, 1968), p. 31. (Hereafter cited as Ridley, *Knox*.)

within his grasp.[4]   There were even suggestions to the effect that other
conservatives such as the questionably assured earl of Bothwell, and the laird of
Buccleuch, would collaborate with Henry by helping him to secure personal
possession of the infant Mary.[5]   Such was the nature of the king's intelligence
which generated an overly optimistic mood among the English during February.

The belief that there had been a closing of ranks between the Scottish
factions, however, was not without some justification.   The only problem, at
least for the English, was the fact that the healing of wounds actually served
Scottish interests and not those of Henry.   The factions had united behind Arran-
-a man who, in spite of the king's opinion, was not so easily manipulated.

The governor's success in convening the Edinburgh parliament on 12
March was indicative of this.   Rumors had circulated that Arran's parliament
would be circumvented by a rival body, summoned by the conservative
followers of Beaton, which was to meet at St. Johnstone's.   The earls of Huntly,
Moray, and Argyle were said to be among the leaders of this movement.   There
was apparently some basis to this report, for on 15 March the Douglas brothers
indicated to Lisle that these earls along with Bothwell and a number of bishops,
abbots, barons, and knights had met in Perth about one week prior to Arran's
parliament.   These men had formulated a number of demands which they
expected the governor to meet: that Beaton should be freed; that the Protestant
gospel should not be preached; that Arran should listen to their advice; and that
the ambassadors chosen by the governor to negotiate with Henry should be
replaced by individuals of their own choosing.   The governor, however, acting

---

[4]*Hamilton Papers*, 1:432, Suffolk, etc., to the privy council, 19 February 1543.

[5]Ibid., and p. 447, Sir Thomas Wharton to Suffolk, etc., 28 February 1543.

upon the advice of the Douglases and his council, refused to grant them these extra-parliamentary and so-called "unreasonable desyres."[6]

Arran had stood firm. The English privy council soon learned that his former colleagues on the cardinal's regency council had given up their intentions to meet independently of his parliament. The report also indicated that the bishops and clergy intended to attend the Edinburgh parliament as they were fearful that Arran's proclivities towards religious reform would harm them.[7] Hence, to the dismay of the English, the governor had succeeded in calling a representative assembly which reflected a cross-section of opinion within his kingdom. Difficult it would be for the pro-English faction to turn the inherent divisiveness of the Scottish nation to their cause's advantage. Regardless of their sympathies, the various factions which convened at Edinburgh were ready to agree on one major point--Scottish independence must be preserved. Henry's designs on Scotland were most definitely beginning to go awry.

In response to the apparent lack of success of the Douglases and the assured Scots in serving his cause, Henry immediately ordered Sir Ralph Sadler to the Scottish capital in an effort to rectify the situation by directly influencing the parliament. The English king must have been confident indeed to believe that one of his own ambassadors actually had the power to accomplish such a feat.

Henry's army may have inflicted severe wounds upon the Scots in battle, but he had by no means turned them into his docile patients. Fear of Henry's

---

[6]*State Papers*, 5:263, Angus and George Douglas to Lisle, 16 March 1542 [sic].

[7]*Hamilton Papers*, 1:458, Suffolk, etc. to the privy council, 8 March 1543; *State Papers*, 5:263-64, Angus and George Douglas to Lisle, 16 March 1542 [sic].

medicine had provided what unity now existed within the northern kingdom.

Addressing Sadler, Henry reminded him of the length of time which had elapsed since Angus, Douglas, and his prisoners had arrived in the northern kingdom. The king had grown impatient and dissatisfied with their conduct. Hence, he desired that Sadler reprimand and whip them into line. Henry had by this time also grown more concerned about the disposition of the various factions within Scotland towards his country. With this in mind, Sadler and a few servants left for Edinburgh where they were to reside until recalled by Henry. Sadler had become the king's key figure in unravelling the complexities and uncertainties of the Scottish situation.[8]

Sadler's instructions of 13 March were to provide the framework for future English policy in regard to Scotland. Although merely hinted at in his instructions, there was no question that the ambassador's primary goal was to prepare the ground for a new regency. Sadler's duplicity was to manifest itself by expressing Henry's favorable opinion of Arran's inclinations while at the same time working to replace the governor with a more amenable Douglas or one of his Solway prisoners. In the king's eyes, Arran was only temporarily ". . . occupieng the place of the Governour." A successful English policy would prove this belief.[9]

The governor, as already emphasized, had succeeded during his early days in office in giving to the English king positive indications that he would be an easy object to overpower. Perhaps this could have proved to be the case had Arran not been so successful in his first parliament. The official

---

[8]Ibid., pp. 261-2, Henry 8 to Sadler, etc., 13 March 1543.

[9]Slavin, *Politics and Profit*, p. 108.

proclamation of the young Hamilton as governor and second person of the realm by a united Scottish assembly, rather than by the select group of lords who had initially called him to his role of leadership, signalled major problems for Henry's plans.

In addition to preventing Arran's confirmation as governor by the parliament, Sadler was to advise the Scottish government on what to instruct their ambassadors commissioned to deal with Henry. They were to be dispatched with instructions in "such playne and certayn termes, as maye be correspondent . . . to his majestes expectacion." Sadler, however, was too late to accomplish either of these objectives.[10]

Upon his arrival at Alnwick in northern England, the ambassador discovered to his dismay that Arran's parliament had already convened and had adjourned until April or May. Unfortunately for Henry, the three estates did not conclude their business before officially approving Arran as governor, petitioning for Beaton's freedom, and drawing up the instructions for their ambassadors who were to be sent to London.

A large part of Sadler's mission had become impossible to achieve, for Scottish diplomatic instructions which he was sent to influence were drafted in such a way as to protect the independence of the northern kingdom. Should an English marriage be arranged, Mary could not be transferred to England-- parliament having declared that she should be left in the possession of her mother and four specially selected Scottish lords. If he chose, however, Henry might send one or two English knights to Scotland and as many ladies of honor

---

[10]*Hamilton Papers*, 1:463, Instructions to Sir Ralph Sadler, 13 March 1543. Only one week after these instructions were given to Henry's ambassador, Arran wrote to the king that he had already commissioned the Scottish negotiators, Royal Ms. 18 B VI folio 152, 20 March 1543.

as he wished with their servants at his own expense. The king was disturbed by these instructions for the Scottish embassy, as the ambassadors did not have the authority to deliver the young queen at his command.[11]

Arran's success in leading such a truly functional Scottish government filled the English with anxiety. On 17 March, Henry's emissary, Suffolk, described this government in apt terms to both the king and his council; ". . . ye shall perceyve the Perliament of Scotlande as it had strange sorte of begynnynge, so to be like to have a straunge endinge."[12] Scottish affairs were becoming increasingly difficult for the English to discern. Sadler realized that the success of the governor was quite contrary to his king's plans of subverting Scottish independence and to his own instructions as Henry's ambassador.

Part of Sadler's instructions, however, were still relevant. He could talk with the Douglases and assured Scots in order to learn more of Scottish affairs and to find those apparently sympathetic to the king's cause. He could also learn why these agents had not fulfilled the promises they had made to the king and why they had been so dilatory in reporting news from Scotland. Next, he

---

[11]*Hamilton Papers*, 1:462, xliii, and 469, Lisle and Sadler to Henry 8, 17 March 1543; *State Papers*, 5:262-5, Angus and George Douglas to Lisle, 16 March 1543; *Sadler's State Papers*, 1:59-63, Sadler's Instructions, 13 March 1543; Great Britain, Public Record Office, *The Acts of the Parliaments of Scotland*, collected by Thomas Thomson and Cosmo Innes, 12 vols. (London: His Majesty's Stationery Office, 1814-75), 2:410 ff. (Hereafter cited as *Acts of the Parliaments*); Great Britain, Public Record Office, *Letters and Papers, Foreign and Domestic, of the Reign of Henry VIII, 1509-47. Preserved in the Public Record Office, the British Museum, and Elsewhere in England*, ed. by Robert H. Brodie and James Gairdner et al, 21 vols. in 33 (London: Her Majesty's Stationery Office, 1901), vol. 18, pt. 1:161-2, Angus and George Douglas to Lisle, 16 March 1543, and pp. 169-74, Sadler to Henry 8, 20 March 1543. (Hereafter cited as *Letters and Papers*); Slavin, *Politics and Profit*, p. 108.

[12]*State Papers*, 5:269, Suffolk, etc. to the council with the king, 17 March 1543. Steven Gunn's *Charles Brandon, Duke of Suffolk c 1484-1545* (Oxford: Blackwell, 1988) is useful.

would sound the queen dowager concerning her views on the future of her infant daughter, as well as ascertaining the inclinations of Arran and other leading personalities.

Following these instructions, Henry emphasized that Sadler was to make it clear that the Scottish ambassadors must satisfy his demands. If the governor gave indications of just dispatching them "with a sleveles errant," or "with thinges of entreteynment," Sadler was to let him know ". . . with whom he hath to do, and what maye ensue of it if it shal appere to the kinges majeste that they goo about to triffle with him." The English ambassador was to report frequently to Henry and Suffolk, and as pointed out in the previous chapter, he was to urge Drummond's replacement of Erskine as secretary of state. Finally, Sadler was to urge Argyle, Moray, Huntly, and others to exhibit a greater conformity to "his majestes most godly purposes," which would be to their advantage considering the strength of the English king.[13]

Henry was a strong king--certainly stronger than Arran was as governor. But unfortunately for the English ruler, the initiative in Anglo-Scottish relations had passed to Arran. Such was the virtually unfathomable nature of the northern kingdom's politics, not yet four months removed from the overwhelming defeat at Solway Moss, the subsequent loss of a king, and the accession of the week-old Mary.

Sadler finally reached Edinburgh on Sunday, 18 March. He was well received by Arran at Holyrood Palace. While there, he was given the opportunity to carry out his instructions of conferring with those named by Henry. Shortly after his arrival, he talked with George Douglas who advised

---

[13]*Hamilton Papers*, 1:462-67, Instructions to Sadler, 13 March 1543.

Henry to be patient and not to attempt too much in so short a time. Of major importance was Douglas's belief that Arran should not be pushed too far. Douglas, by his own admission and those of others as well, exerted a tremendous amount of influence upon the governor. He perceived that whatever the king hoped to accomplish must be done through Arran, unless Henry chose to use force, which was not desirable in the present circumstances.[14] Under no conditions would it be wise for the king to attempt to deprive him of his office, lest a serious reaction ensue. In short, according to Douglas, the nature of the Scottish government was currently beyond the scope of Henry's power to change.

In fact, a large part of the king's Scottish mission had already been set back as early as the first of January when Arran was proclaimed governor. Hence, there was little that the assured Scots could have done to alter that fact once they had arrived. A wiser and more feasible English policy would be the deliverance of Arran and his kingdom from the fold of the Roman church.[15]

Douglas described for Sadler how successfully Arran's parliament had progressed even though at its inception there were those Scots that did ". . . grenne at a nother, yet there was none that wolde byte." Fear of their powerful southern neighbor had provided the occasion for such an unusual and rare display of Scottish cohesion.[16]

In his talks with Sadler, Douglas made it clear that he was not bound by

---

[14]Ibid., pp. 476-77, Sadler to Henry 8, 20 March 1547; *Sadler's State Papers*, 1:68-71, Sadler to Henry 8, 20 March 1543.

[15]Ibid.; *Hamilton Papers*, 1:474-7, Sadler to Henry 8, 20 March 1543.

[16]Ibid., p. 475; *Sadler's State Papers*, 1:67, Sadler to Henry 8, 20 March 1543.

the same oaths as those offered to Henry by the assured lords. In other words, he had never promised to secure Arran's government for the king or to place either the infant queen or the principal fortresses in his majesty's hands.[17]

From such conversation, Sadler understood that Henry's designs on Scotland were at that time virtually impossible to achieve. Other agents of Henry's cause concurred with Douglas's assessment of the situation. Yet, despite this, Angus and Glencairn still gave the English king some encouragement. They reinforced the idea that Arran was ". . . a very gentle creature and a symple man easie to be ruled."[18] Even the conservative Bothwell, who had fallen out with the governor for his own personal reasons, approached Sadler, informing him of his desire to serve Henry. Bothwell, however, once again confirmed the idea that the assured Scots would not be immediately able to satisfy their promises in spite of the head of the Scottish government ". . . who is more mete to be governed then to be a governour."[19] Regardless of such negative opinions of Arran, Douglas's assessment of Scottish politics was correct. The English must plan to concentrate their efforts around the earl's role as lawful governor.

Sadler's initial conversation with the governor centered around the future of the cardinal. The apparent lack of confidence which the ambassador expressed concerning Scotland's new government was illustrative of earlier English attempts, before Arran's official proclamation by parliament, to push him into Henry's camp. Sadler predicted that if the cardinal were set free, he

---

[17]Ibid., pp. 68-9; *Hamilton Papers*, 1:476, Sadler to Henry 8, 20 March 1543.

[18]Ibid., p. 480; *Sadler's State Papers*, 1:75, Sadler to Henry 8, 20 March 1543.

[19]Ibid., pp.81; *Hamilton Papers*, 1:484-5, Sadler to Henry 8, 20 March 1543.

would not only usurp Arran's position as governor but would seek to destroy him and the entire Scottish realm out of his love for France. Sadler went so far as to describe Beaton as "better French than Scottish."[20] In response to this denunciation of the cardinal, Arran remarked, ". . . he shall never cum out of pryson whilles I lyve, except it be to his further mischiefe."[21]

The governor, as his contemporaries believed, was weak in some respects. Yet, out of such weakness came two important but related characteristics--insincerity and vacillation. As regards Anglo-Scottish relations, these traits completely perplexed the English in trying to decipher Arran's actual attitude or position on any given issue. Such characteristics in dealing with a king like Henry were not bad. The insincerity and vacillation of the governor served the Scots' interests well because from them evolved a significant temporizing policy with the king which greatly undercut the English position in Scotland.[22]

Sadler proceeded by meeting with the queen dowager on 22 March at Linlithgow. Confirming earlier reports, she indicated her willingness to consent to the proposed English marriage, desiring that the young queen be taken to England for protection from Arran, who she thought wanted her daughter to marry his own son. The queen dowager stated that Arran had no true intention of marrying the young Mary to the English prince, as he was merely practicing duplicity with the king. All that the governor wanted to do was to make the contract, keeping the queen until her lawful age in hopes that during the

---

[20]Ibid., pp. 481-2; *Sadler's State Papers*, 1:74-7, Sadler to Henry 8, 20 March 1543.

[21]Ibid., p. 77; *Hamilton Papers*, 1:482, Sadler to Henry 8, 20 March 1543.

[22]Ibid., xliv.

meantime Henry might die. Thus, the Scots would be given the opportunity to break the treaty commitments with his demise. Arran was anxious to keep Mary in Scotland as it was only by her authority that he was able to act. Mary of Guise maintained that the present Scottish government believed that if its queen died in England, Henry would have someone replace her at home. Arran's government also seemed to believe, according to the queen dowager, that if the English prince died, Mary would be married to another person of Henry's choosing. In short, regardless of the course of events, the English king would be able to dispose of Scotland as he saw fit provided he got his way concerning the marriage.

Mary of Guise even went so far as to state if Beaton were freed, he too would pursue Henry's views. Upon hearing such speculation, Sadler might well have suspected that there was no longer a French party within Scotland. For here was the major proponent of the Guise faction within Scotland abandoning what influence her homeland had over the northern kingdom in favor of the English cause. Sadler was confused, but so was Scottish politics. Continuing to calm English suspicions, the queen dowager maintained that she had no intention to marry the earl of Lennox and that there was no truth whatsoever to the report that her father, the duke of Guise, was coming to Scotland at the head of an army. Finally, she showed Sadler her young namesake who lay "naked in her nursery"--a fine specimen of a young queen.[23]

In the same correspondence in which he reported his audience with the queen dowager, Sadler relayed the message from George Douglas that Cardinal

---

[23]Ibid., p. 488, Sadler to Henry 8, 23 March 1543; *Sadler's State Papers*, 1:84-8, Sadler to Henry 8, 23 March 1543; *Letters and Papers*, vol. 18, pt. 1:177-8, Sadler to Henry 8, 23 March 1543.

Beaton might be moved from Blackness, his latest place of confinement, to St. Andrews, his own home. When the English later discovered that this had occurred, they were not pleased, especially in view of assurances to the contrary made by the governor shortly before. Beaton had been given virtual freedom by this transfer. Such was the character of Scottish politics--or more accurately, the character of Arran.[24]

In regard to the prelate, the king and his council instructed Sadler to do all that he could to have him transferred to a point as near the English border as was possible. There Beaton could easily be brought into Henry's personal possession.[25]

Henry became increasingly intolerant of the Scottish situation. Arran, in spite of his alleged simplicity, was clearly not functioning in accord with the king's desires and plans. Henry's recommendation that Drummond be confirmed as the Scottish secretary of state was ignored. The office instead went to Henry Balnavis, one of the governor's ambassadors to England. Likewise, the bishop of Glasgow regained his position as chancellor following Beaton's imprisonment, Henry's choice of the earl of Glencairn being overlooked. Thus, the English king's goal to infiltrate the Scottish government with a set of puppets was set back by these major developments.[26]

Henry's dissatisfaction with the Douglases and assured Scots continued to mount. He instructed Sadler to threaten them as a result of the failure to

---

[24]*Hamilton Papers*, 1:488, Sadler to Henry 8, 23 March 1543; *Sadler's State Papers*, 1:88-90, Sadler to Henry 8, 23 March 1543.

[25]*Hamilton Papers*, 1:491, the privy council to Sadler, 25 March 1543.

[26]Ibid., p. 492, Sadler to Henry 8, 27 March 1543; *Sadler's State Papers*, 1:90-1, Sadler to Henry 8, 27 March 1543.

fulfill their pledges and inefficiency in reporting the news of Scotland to him. Henry's bitterest complaint, however, was the fact that these agents allowed the Scottish parliament by a special act to frustrate his designs of subjugating the political independence of that kingdom. This was done by the "unmete" Arran having been officially proclaimed as governor and second person within their realm. The assured Scots' assertion that this was an accomplished fact even before their arrival fell on deaf ears.[27]

It appears that Henry placed a large part of the blame for the cardinal's release on George Douglas.[28] Douglas, however, maintained that he alone kept Arran loyal to Henry and instead placed the blame for the apparent instability of the governor on the earl of Huntly, whom he described as "the falsest and wylyest yong man a lyve."[29]

Douglas had attempted to prevail upon the governor to reverse his attitude on Beaton's detention. On April Fool's Day, an apt day for the governor in more ways than one, Arran vowed to Sadler that he would never allow the cardinal to leave "prison" so long a he lived. Arran made it very clear, however, that he would not consent to the cardinal's transfer to England. In fact, Beaton had been taken to St. Andrews in order that a papal interdict might be removed so that mass could be celebrated by the priests in the various

---

[27]Ibid., pp. 101-3, Henry 8 to Sadler, 30 March 1543; *Hamilton Papers*, 1:494-5, Henry 8 to Sadler, 30 March 1943.

[28]Ibid., p. 494; *Sadler's State Papers*, 1:101-2, Henry 8 to Sadler, 30 March 1543.

[29]Ibid., pp. 104-8, Sadler to the privy council, 31 March 1543; *Hamilton Papers*, 1:496, Sadler to the privy council, 31 March 1543.

churches at Easter.[30]

Why was the governor so obstinate on this particular point? In part, instead of seeing the cardinal as merely a domestic political opponent, Arran viewed him also as a religious threat. Once again, the governor reaffirmed in his 1 April conversation with Sadler his commitment to the Protestant cause as defined by Henry. If he were surrendered to the English king, Beaton would no doubt cease to be a political threat to the governor at home. The cardinal's surrender, however, would court further alienation and hostility from those masses of people in Scotland who already resented his imprisonment and whose religious consciences Arran still had hopes of reforming. As such, the governor was in a better position if Beaton were kept at home.

Of greater significance to Arran than even his religious proclivities was his desire to preserve Scottish independence from the designs of his southern neighbor. Henry's religion appealed to the governor; his politics did not. Arran, for example, knew that the deliverance of Beaton to the English would be viewed by many Scots as an overt action working directly against their nation's sovereignty by fitting all too well with Henry's wishes. Political and religious differences would persist during the next few months between the cardinal and the governor. Yet, they were never so strong as to force even a trimmer like Arran to bow to English demands that he surrender his major rival.

In this same conversation, Sadler also discovered that at least part of what Mary of Guise had told him concerning the governor's desire to see his own son marry the young queen of Scotland was true. In fact, the queen

---

[30]Ibid., p. 497, Sadler to the privy council, 1 April 1543; *Sadler's State Papers*, 1:108-12, Sadler to the privy council, 1 April 1543; *Letters and Papers*, vol. 18, pt. 1:202-3, Sadler to the privy council, 1 April 1543.

dowager had even agreed to the plan herself. But as Arran pointed out, as soon as he learned about the proposal of the English marriage from Henry's paroled prisoners, he decided to pursue the king's desire with all his power. According to the governor, it was Mary of Guise's intent ". . . to set the king and himself 'at pyke,' and to release the cardinal." The queen dowager, wanting to enhance her own political fortunes at the expense of Arran, saw the advantage of Henry's insistence upon the immediate custody of her young daughter. No matter how obliging the governor was, Arran could never consent to such action, as it was a clear threat to Scottish sovereignty.[31] His surrender of Beaton to the English would likewise bring his national loyalties into suspicion.

The day after this revealing conversation with Arran, Sadler paid another visit to Mary of Guise at Linlithgow. She persisted in her assertion that Arran was of one mind regarding her daughter's marriage--it must be to his son. Although she still desired that the young queen be sent to England for protection against the governor's designs, she realized that few of the Scottish lords would agree to that. In addition, the queen dowager, like many others, continued to complain of Arran's inconstancy.

As a result of this series of conversations, the English ambassador grew tremendously bewildered. Who could be trusted? Sadler, guided by religious sympathies, decided to place his confidence in the one personality who seemed most faithful to the Protestant cause--the governor. For the English envoy, the word of one good Protestant far outweighed those of many good Catholics,

---

[31]*Sadler's State Papers*, 1:114-15 and 111-12, Sadler to the privy council, 1 April 1543; *Hamilton Papers*, 1:497, Sadler to the privy council, 1 April 1543.

Mary of Guise included.[32]

Concluding his report to the privy council, Sadler made a seemingly simple request which was to have profound consequences later upon his king's Scottish policy and the direction of Arran's regency. He asked the council to urge Henry to return to Scotland the abbot of Paisley, one of the governor's illegitimate brothers. Arran desperately wanted Paisley at his side, leading Sadler to remark that the abbot might be a replacement for Beaton at St. Andrews.[33]

Henry's attitude at this stage of diplomatic relations between the two kingdoms coincided with that of his emissaries closer to the central arena of Scottish affairs. The king would continue to follow a policy of gentle measures, especially in regard to Arran. The English party should encourage the governor in those areas where he showed positive inclinations of following Henry. In spite of Arran's attitude on other matters, the English king was pleased with his desire to further the Protestant cause. Hence, Henry offered Sadler directions on how to cultivate this propensity, quite likely, in hopes of bringing the governor under his political influence as well. The ambassador was to promise Arran the king's book of "pure true doctrine" composed with both "labour and paynes" as soon as it was finished.[34]

Sadler was also to show the governor how to handle the church, in particular, its lands, abbeys, monks, and friars, by the use of commissioners. A

---

[32]Ibid., Sadler to the privy council, 2 April 1543; *Sadler's State Papers*, 1:113-17, Sadler to the privy council, 2 April 1543; Slavin, *Politics and Profit*, p. 113.

[33]*Hamilton Papers*. 1:497, Sadler to the privy council, 2 April 1543; *Sadler's State Papers*, 1:117, Sadler to the privy council, 2 April 1543.

[34]*Hamilton Papers*, 1:499, Henry 8 to Sadler, 4 April 1543.

few days later, Arran agreed with the English king's views on the scriptures. Yet, according to the governor, the abolition of monks and friars and the cutting off of connections with Rome would be a particularly arduous task within Scotland. Regardless of this, it was a responsibility which Arran showed a willingness to bear. He held that all religious houses were initially founded to pray for souls in purgatory, the existence of which he could not accept. As such, these establishments were vain, and there was little doubt that they could be put to better use.[35]

Finally, and most significantly of all in respect to the governor, the king moved to the topic of marriage--not the prince's marriage, but the marriage of Arran's son to his youngest daughter, Princess Elizabeth. The king was pleased that the governor had immediately given up whatever desire he once had to marry his son to the young Scottish queen on learning of Henry's plans to have her wed Prince Edward. To show the gratitude for Arran's willingness to further the English cause at his own expense, Henry offered Arran the ". . . wayes and meanes for the avauncement of the reputacion of his bloude as he may have cause to rejoyse and take comforte in his conformitie to our procedinges."[36] Henry informed Sadler that, although there was nothing publicly said against Arran, the governor should be warned that there were "pryve muttrynges and wysperynges specially agaynst hym" which might eventually erupt into the open. To protect himself, Arran would do well to agree to such a proposal with the one condition that he seal it, or show his

---

[35]Ibid., pp. 499-500; *Letters and Papers*, vol. 18, pt. 1:229-31, Sadler to Henry 8, 9 April 1543; *Sadler's State Papers*, 1:127-9, Sadler to Henry 8, 9 April 1543.

[36]*Hamilton Papers*, 1:501, Henry 8 to Sadler, 4 April 1543.

benevolence, by sending his son to live at the English court. This, according to Henry, was ". . . the oonly waye and meane for the governour to kepe his place and estabylish his bloude in suertye."[37] Continuing to press this point, the king maintained that Arran's power as regent would last only until Mary reached her majority. By consenting to this marriage, however, a perpetual honor and security would be given to both him and his family.[38]

Henry told Sadler that Arran was to discuss this proposal of marriage between their two children with just a few of "his most trusty freindes," if he did not immediately accept it.[39] Certainly, the sincerity of the king's offer must be questioned. Most likely it was just another of his attempts to make the governor his chief puppet. But Arran, in spite of his alleged weakness, vanity, and susceptibility, was not so stupid. He put the king off by stating that when the treaty between their two kingdoms was settled, which would soon take place unless Henry sought to destroy Scottish sovereignty, he would agree to the marriage of his son to the English princess.[40] The governor's temporizing policy had once again manifested itself.

Arran suspected that the English king was already at work on the border to undermine his position within Scotland.[41] A cautious Douglas warned

---

[37]Ibid., p. 502.

[38]Ibid.

[39]Ibid.

[40]*Sadler's State Papers*, 1:129 and 136-42, Sadler to Henry 8, 12 April 1543; *Letters and Papers*, vol. 18, pt. 1:231-33, Sadler to Henry 8, 12 April 1543.

[41]*Hamilton Papers*, 1:xliv and 516, Sadler to the privy council, 18 April 1543.

Sadler of threatening the inconstant governor. According to Douglas, the king's party should continue its pretense of supporting the governour as well as the "common wealthe" of Scotland, for if Arran knew that Henry intended to take control of the northern kingdom, he would immediately embrace the cardinal's pro-French faction. In addition, Douglas maintained that ". . . the hole realme wooll stand fast with hym, and dye rather all in a daye, then they woolde be made thrall and subject of England."[42]

The French threat continued to become more apparent to the English. On 6 April Sadler reported to the king that the earl of Lennox had peaceably landed at Dumbarton with two ships and a small retinue with enough money ". . . that Fraunce woolde now fyll theyr Scottyshe purses with golde."[43] In addition to the money, Lennox had brought "many fayre woordes and lesynges oute of Fraunce" by which he would attempt to allure as many Scotsmen as he could to their devotion and party.[44] Henry's emissaries had been confused far enough by the Scots themselves. France, however, had now chosen to add to that bewilderment by its reinvolvement in the concerns of its partner in "the auld alliance." "Perplexed," indeed, was the state of affairs in Scotland during this momentous year. Arran himself was even at his "'wits' end'" concerning the recent events and developments there.[45]

---

[42]Ibid., p. 505, conversation with Douglas reported by Sadler to Henry 8, 6 April 1543.

[43]Ibid., pp. 510-11, Sadler to Henry 8, 6 April 1543.

[44]Ibid., 511.

[45]Ibid., p. 512, Sadler to Henry 8, 9 April 1543; *Sadler's State Papers*, 1:127-35, Sadler to Henry 8, 9 April 1543; *Letters and Papers*, vol. 18, pt. 1:229-30, Sadler to Henry 8, 9 April 1543.

On 12 April, Sadler conveyed the information that Lennox was still in the west where his movements were as yet uncertain.[46] He also reported to Henry on another interview which he had with Arran. The governor had acknowledged the honor shown him by Henry's proposal to marry Elizabeth to his son, and had sworn many great oaths concerning his innocence in the release of Beaton.[47]

Henry remained anxious concerning the complexities and uncertainties of the Scottish situation. French intervention had altered affairs considerably. The unstable Arran could perhaps be brought just as easily into their fold as Henry could win him to his side. Who knew what to expect when dealing with a man of the governor's character? One faulty move by the English and their designs on Scotland would be destroyed. The unreasonable pursuance of Henry's plan would make untenable the position of his assured agents who would ". . . be left alone and dryven to flye into England."[48]

Henry's scheme depended on the actions of the governor. On 13 April, the privy council wrote to Sadler urging him to warn Arran against the French threat to his rule, specifically emphasizing the fear that Lennox and Beaton would try to gain possession of the young queen. Sadler should make it known to the governor that she must be brought to Edinburgh Castle for protection against their devious designs.[49] Douglas, however, cautioned against making

---

[46]*Hamilton Papers*, 1:512, Sadler to Henry 8, 12 April 1543; *Sadler's State Papers*, 1:140, Sadler to Henry 8, 12 April 1543.

[47]Ibid., pp. 136-9; *Hamilton Papers*, 1:512, Sadler to Henry 8, 12 April 1543.

[48]Ibid., p. 511, Sadler to Henry 8, 6 April 1543.

[49]Ibid., p. 513, the privy council to Sadler, 13 April 1543.

such suggestions to Arran because they might increase his already obvious suspicions and fears concerning Henry's Scottish policy.[50] Nevertheless, Sadler obeyed the instructions sent to him by his king's council. Arran explained to him that the young Mary was perfectly safe at Linlithgow with her French mother. Linlithgow and Stirling had been chosen as her royal residences by his parliament.[51] The governor, who tended to give, at least superficially, the impression of being as accommodating as possible, had no objection to having her moved to Edinburgh where her father had been reared. The other lords would probably agree with him, although he stated that he did not know the inclination of the queen's mother on this subject.[52]

Arran's lack of cooperation with the English was beginning to disturb them. As the Scottish governor played for time, Henry VIII became more upset. Procrastination and frustration became one and the same in this delicate situation of Anglo-Scottish relations.

---

[50]Ibid., p. 516, Sadler to the privy council, 18 April 1543.

[51]Ibid.

[52]Ibid., p. 518.

CHAPTER IV

An Accord Seemingly Secured:
The Treaties of Greenwich

April 1543 was a very significant month in the history of Anglo-Scottish relations. Failure of the Scots to see eye to eye with the English in negotiating the treaties of peace and marriage played a large role in the mounting tension between the two kingdoms. Arran's conduct in office had much to do with this rapidly intensifying situation.

The exaggerated political claims of Henry VIII conflicted with the rights of the governor, next in line to the Scottish throne after Mary. In one of his many dispatches to Sadler, Henry made clear his concept of suzerainty over Scotland by his description of a phase of the negotiations:

> There was summe reasoning betwene them and our counsail, in the debating of this matyer, touchinge our title to Scotland, which was spoken by reason of a request they made that, if She shuld dye without issue, the realme shuld remayne to the next heire of bludde there, whereby they wold have had Us made an entayll, which shuld have ymplyed a graunte that there rested in Us no right to that realme. But it was soo quickely cast of, and our title so vively repeted, that that martyer fell, and finally they desired to have our resolution in writing, offering to

goo with it, or to sende it, for the more expedition, and better framing of all thinges to purpose. Which We granted, and therupon delyvered them a scedule, the copy wherof you shall receve, to thintent you maye in expresse wordes joyne with them in the matyer of the same.[1]

In the same correspondence with Sadler, the king outlined this schedule of what he expected from the Scots in the important treaties then being negotiated. These demands were expressed in three major articles. In the first, Henry was willing to offer the infant Mary a dowry as great as that ever received by an English queen--provided that after the contract of marriage with his son had been made she be brought within his kingdom to be educated. If, however, her tender age required delay, hostages should be sent for her delivery within two years. These hostages would show the Scots' good faith in regard to the observation of the treaties' terms.[2]

This demand was more than the Scottish ambassadors appointed by Arran's parliament, namely, James Learmouth, William Hamilton, and Henry Balnavis, were instructed to meet. The principal provision carried by these men to London was that Mary must reside in Scotland until she was able to consummate her marriage, or was at least ten years of age. Hostages were to be offered for her delivery at that time. Also, should Edward die before Mary and there were no children of the marriage, she was to be brought back to

---

[1]*State Papers*, 5:279, Henry 8 to Sadler, 14 April 1543.

[2]Ibid., pp. 271-80; *Hamilton Papers*, 1:ci-cii, Answers to the ambassadors of Scotland, April 1543.

Scotland where she could marry a man of her choosing.[3] While these Scottish ambassadors were empowered to contract the marriage, it had to be confirmed by their parliament. All the Scottish nobles also had to ". . . yeve their seals" for its implementation.[4]

Henry's second demand provided for a perpetual peace which he would make upon the conclusion of the terms of marriage. The treaty was to be based upon the idea, "frende to frende, and ennemye to ennemy." Hence, Scotland's traditional alliance with France would be severed.[5]

The third article on the king's schedule concerned Arran's government. If he continued in devotion to Henry, Arran would be allowed to remain in office as governor during Mary's minority and perhaps even after it, should he prove himself worthy. He would also be permitted to enjoy all the revenues of the Scottish kingdom except that which was needed for Mary's education. The whole article, however, was contingent upon the fact that Arran would heed the advice of those people whom Henry deemed best suited as counsellors.[6]

The final demand subordinated Arran's government to that of Henry. Such an article understandably would be difficult for the Scottish negotiators to accept. In fact, their parliament had instructed them in no uncertain terms to protect Arran's authority and rights:

---

[3]*Sadler's State Papers*, 1:59-63, Instructions for contracting the peace and marriage, 13; March 1543; also *Acts of the Parliaments*, 2:410-13 and *Letters and Papers*, vol. 18, pt. 1:155-6.

[4]*State Papers*, 5:276-7, Henry 8 to Sadler, 14 April 1543.

[5]Ibid.; *Hamilton Papers*, 1:ci-cii, Answers to the ambassadors of Scotland, April 1543.

[6]Ibid.; *State Papers*, 5:278, Henry 8 to Sadler, 14 April 1543.

> . . . That in caiss the quenis grace our soverane lady cummis to
> perfite aige, and passis furth of the realme, it is to be desirit, that
> my lord governour that now is, remane governour of thys realme
> for all the dayis of his lif, and efter his deceiss, that the narrest
> lauchful of his blude, abill to succede, and to exerce the said
> office, salbe maid governour of the realme be out said soverane
> lady and hir successouris succedand to the crone of Ingland, be
> large and ample commission, of the quhilk the form is to be
> deviste.[7]

On 19 April, Sadler reported to his king that the governor seemed
adverse to the propositions outlined for Scottish acceptance.[8] Arran's desire to
accommodate himself with Henry began to waver noticeably. The following
day, Sadler had yet another interview with the governor who expressed his
complete dissatisfaction with Henry's demands, saying that ". . . he could not
be induced, nor perswaded to condescend unto the same."[9]

At this point in Arran's regency, two profound influences upon his career
coalesced. Particularly important in Arran's change of behavior towards the
English was the return of his natural brother, John Hamilton, the abbot of
Paisley. According to Sadler, the governor had fallen under his complete
domination.[10] The abbot, a future archbishop of St. Andrews, was a man of

---

[7]*Sadler's State Papers*, 1:62, Instructions for contracting the peace and marriage, 13 March
1543; also *Acts of the Parliaments*, 2:412.

[8]*Sadler's State Papers*, 1:147, Sadler to Henry 8, 19 April 1543; *Hamilton Papers*, 1:520-1,
Sadler to Henry 8, 19 April 1543.

[9]Ibid., 1:522, Sadler to Henry 8, 20 April 1543; *Sadler's State Papers*, 1:152-6, Sadler to
Henry 8, 20 April 1543.

[10]Ibid., 1:145, Sadler to Henry 8, 19 April 1543; *Hamilton Papers*, 1:520-1, Sadler to Henry
8, 19 April 1543.

tremendous ambition who had attached himself to Beaton. Hence, he did all within his power to bring the susceptible Arran into supporting the Catholic cause. The other influence was the question of his own legitimacy. In attempting to win the governor over to Beaton's side, the abbot argued that questions concerning his father's divorce from Elizabeth Home would undoubtedly threaten Arran's own rule and claim to the Scottish succession should he completely sever his ties with Rome. Among Henry's friends, the earl of Glencairn summed up much of what Paisley maintained was being said about the governor. The earl held that Arran was unwise, inconstant, and lacking in political acumen. In addition to these qualities, the governor had no title to the crown of Scotland, for he was unquestionably a bastard. In short, because of paternal matters, it was best that Arran be on friendly terms with the Roman church which had the power to undo him.[11]

The extent to which the abbot attempted to reconcile the governor with Beaton is well illustrated by the fact that he was the instrument whereby Arran bargained a simoniacal transaction with the cardinal. By this agreement, Arran's son was to receive a church pension amounting to one thousand pounds per year for the rest of his life. This deal, however, was contingent upon the young Hamilton entering into holy orders. The full details of this agreement were yet

---

[11]Ibid., and pp. 522-23, Sadler to Henry 8, 20 April 1543 and 22 April 1543; *Sadler's State Papers*, 1:157, Sadler to Henry 8, 20 April 1543 and pp. 158 and 160, Sadler to Henry 8, 22 April 1543; William Anderson, *The Scottish Nation: or the Surnames, Families, Literature, Honours and Biographical History of the People of Scotland*, 3 vols. (Edinburgh: A. Fullarton and Col, 1863), 2:430-1; Knox, *History*, 1:49-50; *Historical Manuscripts Commission, Eleventh Report*, p. 49; *Dictionary of National Biography*, s.v. "Hamilton, James, Second Earl of Arran and Duke of Châtelheuralt," by Robert Dunlop.

unknown to the English party.[12]

Arran's strongest ties with Henry's cause, his genuine proclivities toward religious reform, were beginning to be checked. Now the governor had a large monetary stake in the situation should he be loyal to Rome. Scottish affairs grew increasingly complicated.

Alongside Paisley and his reminder of Arran's questionable legitimacy was the harshness of Henry's demands which help account for the governor's vacillating and unpredictable behavior.[13] Arran's conduct so intrigued the king's party that both Douglases and a number of the assured lords were impelled to act decisively in hopes of keeping the governor closer to the English position than that of the pro-French party.[14]

In late April, Arran nearly defected to Henry's opposition. The governor silenced his friar preachers, Thomas Gwilliam and John Rough, and summoned Beaton and the rest of the French party to his side.[15] At this point, George Douglas resolved that Arran was so fickle and inconstant that no more promises could be made concerning the governor or his attitude toward Henry's demands. According to Douglas, the governor's overtures toward Beaton's camp had compromised the English king's position for that party would never agree to

---

[12]Slavin, *Politics and Profit*, p. 118; R. K. Hannay, Jane Harvey, and Marguerite Woods, "Some Papal Bulls among the Hamilton Papers," *Scottish Historical Review*, 22 (1924), 39.

[13]*Sadler's State Papers*, 1:152-6, Sadler to Henry 8, 20 April 1543; *Hamilton Papers*, 1:522, Sadler to Henry 8, 20 April 1543.

[14]*Sadler's State Papers*, 1:160-1, Sadler to Henry 8, 26 April 1543; also in *Letters and Papers*, vol. 18, pt. 1:272-4.

[15]*Hamilton Papers*, 1:522-3, Sadler to Henry 8, 22 April 1543; *Sadler's State Papers*, 1:158-60, Sadler to Henry 8, 22 April 1543; *Letters and Papers*, vol. 18, pt. 1:267, footnote.

anything aimed against themselves or France. Neither would they consent to the young queen's quick delivery--both major items among the king's requests.[16]

Henry's attempt to deal with the Scots following his victory at Solway Moss was now transformed from what seemed a basically Anglo-Scottish affair into one of international proportions. Although quite successful at frustrating and baffling the English king, Arran was no military match for Henry. Francis I, however, by intervening in Scottish affairs, could quickly change that inequality. The French king wanted Arran's government to maintain its traditional alliance with his country. According to a report brought by Lennox, Francis stated that he would uphold this alliance with the Scots should the English king attempt an invasion. Men, money, and munitions would be sent to combat this aggression. Concerning the items being negotiated with the English, Francis desired that if some agreement were reached, the Scots would at least comprehend or make provisions for him in the league and treaty made. Such information was disconcerting to the English party as it was known that the Scots could expect aid from Denmark as well.[17]

Henry's repeated threats to use force had now lost some of their bite.

---

[16]*Sadler's State Papers*, 1:158-60, Sadler to Henry 8, 22 April 1543; *Hamilton Papers*, 1:522-3, Sadler to Henry 8, 22 April 1543.

[17]Ibid., 1:519, Sadler to Suffolk and Tunstall, 18 April 1543; *Sadler's State Papers*, 1:160-3, Sadler to Henry 8, 26 April 1543. Concerning the secondary Danish alliance see *Hamilton Papers*, 1:lxxi, a memorandum by a spy, *circa* 16 November 1542 and Royal Ms. 18 B VI folio 154, Mary Queen of Scots to Christian 3, 10 June 1543. Two other almost illegible documents pertinent to Danish-Scottish relations are found in the Royal Ms. 18 B VI folio 58b, Christian 3 to Arran, 27 March 1543 and folio 59b, Arran to Christian 3, April [1543]. Also, Annie Isabella.Cameron, ed., *The Warrender Papers*, 2 vols., Scottish History Society Publications, third series, vols. 18 and 19 (Edinburgh: University Press, 1931), 18:8-14. (Hereafter cited as *Warrender Papers*.) Also *Letters and Papers*, vol. 19, pt. 1:458, Christian 3 to Mary Queen of Scots, 21 June 1544 for response.

Hence, new instructions were dispatched to Sadler on 25 April. Because of delicate circumstances, the English king persisted in appealing directly to the governor where he felt that he was most susceptible--the reminder that he would surely lose power if he changed sides. The tone of these latest directions to Sadler betrayed a sense of desperation on Henry's part.[18]

The earl of Lennox, who had refused to ratify Arran's appointment as governor, remained a political threat to him. Questions concerning his legitimacy were heard more frequently. Arran, however, displayed much confidence concerning his superiority over his rival. He reported to Sadler in early May that he was resolved to deal quickly with Lennox for his refusal to recognize the Hamilton's claim to the Scottish succession as well as his failure to deliver Dumbarton Castle.[19]

The day after Henry had sent him his latest instructions, Sadler wrote to his king describing how the assured lords' influence upon the governor had paid off. Arran, described now as being in "a good towardness," would agree to at least part of what the king wanted provided Henry would only relent somewhat. From various conferences with Cassillis, Glencairn, Maxwell, and Somerville, Sadler became convinced that Arran would agree to pledges for Mary's delivery when she was of lawful age.

Regarding Scotland's bond with Henry's continental foe, Sadler reported the rumor that ". . . the whole realm murmereth that they had rather die than

---

[18]*Hamilton Papers*, 1:527-8, Henry 8 to Sadler, 25 April 1543. See Appendix III.

[19]Ibid., 1:529, Sadler to Suffolk, 28 April 1543 and p. 533, Sadler to Suffolk, Tunstall, and Parr, 5 May 1543 and Sadler to the privy council, 6 May 1543; *Sadler's State Papers*, 1:184-6, Sadler to Suffolk, Durham, and Parr, 5 May 1543 and 1:188-9, Sadler to the privy council, 6 May 1543.

break their old leagues with France." The ambassador did maintain, however, that the Scots would perhaps join in an amity whereby France would not actually benefit from "the auld alliance." At this time, Sadler was desperately looking for any optimistic lead he could find. For upon such, to use Sadler's metaphor, a foundation might be built whereby Henry would see his ultimate designs realized.

The other demand of the king, however, seemed less likely to be realized. The Scots would not agree to Arran's counsellors being chosen by Henry, as that seemed to establish an English council in their kingdom.[20]

Henry now had two choices--to relent on the severity of his demands or to use outright force, thereby risking the consequences of such action with the Scots' continental allies. Arran had been pushed almost too far by the English king. The possible repercussions of such action coupled with the influence of the abbot of Paisley upon him were ominous to English success. The king's plan had to be modified.

Actually, Henry used a combination of the two alternatives available to him. He quickly reduced the schedule of demands for the treaty but continued to give the impression that he would resort to force should this revised plan not be accepted. The communications with Lord Parr, who was the new warden of the marches, Suffolk, and others of the English party indicate that Henry was willing to go to this extreme.[21]

---

[20]Ibid., 1:160-4, Sadler to Henry 8, 26 April 1543; also in *Letters and Papers*, vol. 18, pt. 1:272-4.

[21]Beer, *Northumberland*, p. 19; *Letters and Papers*, vol. 18, pt. 1:276, Henry 8 to Suffolk, 28 April 1543; *State Papers*, 5:266-68, instructions to Parr, 1543 and p. 280, the privy council to Sadler, 1 May 1543.

On 1 May the privy council informed Sadler of the king's new position. Although Henry marvelled that Arran could be at such odds with his intial demands, he was still anxious to come to terms with the governor. Sadler was instructed to make it known to the English party that unless they induced the governor and others in authority to agree to the modified schedule without further alteration, Henry would resort to force to insure the success of his enterprise.[22]

The king requested that three earls, three bishops, and two barons be delivered to him as pledges of the Scots' word in keeping the following provisions of the treaty: the first article provided for the actual marriage between Edward and Mary. The major change from the initial demand was the provision that the queen be delivered to the English when she was at most ten years of age. The conditions that Mary be kept by both English and Scottish attendants and at places prescribed by Henry for her "suerty and healthe" were also stated.[23]

The second point insured a "perfite amytie and perpetual peax" described once again as, "freende to freende, and enemye to enemye" with the renunciation of the Scots' amity with the French. Also a pact was to be created whereby the Scots would not enter into "amytie" with any other "Prince, state, or Potentate" thereafter without the English sovereign's consent. Likewise, Henry would not make a league with any other sovereign unless the Scots were included in the pact. The Scots were also to aid and assist the English monarch for reasonable

---

[22]Ibid., privy council to Sadler.

[23]Ibid., p. 281.

wages against all other rulers regardless of who they were.[24]

The third article once again directly concerned Arran. He would be recognized as the governor during the queen's minority provided that ". . . he contynue his good devotion and inclynation towardes the Kinges Majestie that he pretendeth." Once more, this was modified by the condition that Arran would also heed the advice of such Scots appointed by the king "to be of counsail with him." Regarding the profits and revenues of the northern kingdom, Henry was satisfied that Arran should have them, provided that a portion should be reserved for the entertainment of the queen and ". . . for such other incident charges as folowe of the same and of this treatye."[25]

As soon as these new demands had been formulated, the governor and a group of the Scottish nobility made their response to the king's original articles. The Scottish assembly had polarized into two distinct parties; the first was the English party to which Arran now seemed wholly committed and for which at least he could gather some support; the second party was composed of the kirkmen and led by the conservative Bothwell who was now opposed to making a treaty with Henry, preferring war instead. To this anti-English party, both peace and unity were anathema, for they were synonymous with reform.[26]

Douglas was the king's strongest supporter in keeping his fellow Scots in line. Sadler reported that it was Douglas alone who had kept the governor from deserting completely to the other party and that it was impossible for any

---

[24]Ibid.

[25]Ibid., pp. 281-2.

[26]*Sadler's State Papers*, 1:168-75, Sadler to Henry 8, 1 May 1543; *Hamilton Papers*, 1:530-1, Sadler to Henry 8, 1 May 1543.

one Scot to have done more to bring Henry's desires to fruition. Therefore, the wrath and hatred of the clergy were especially directed against him.[27]

Sadler had again discussed the king's original demands with Arran and some of the other nobles, urging acceptance. He met with limited success. The governor blamed the kirkmen for making it impossible for him to meet all of Henry's demands. Also, according to Arran, the king earlier had erred in trying to win the independent minded Bothwell to his side. For now, the earl was opposed to all and ". . . would forsake Scotland, France, and England, for ever, rather than he would consent to lay pledges for the performance of the marriage." In spite of this, the governor had brought the nobility to resolve that it would be better to give pledges than to have war. Hence, Henry should have them as a sign of good faith for the marriage and their queen's deliverance "within a year or two of her lawful age."[28]

Arran was now reported to be so desirous of the treaties that he had agreed to the marriage between Henry's daughter Elizabeth and his own son. This led Douglas to describe the governor's son, who by his own right might one day be king of Scotland should Mary die, as the best possible pledge Henry could hope to have.[29]

Regarding the peace, Arran said that the nobility had remained so close to their old alliance with France that he could not persuade them to accept Henry's demand regarding the friend to friend and enemy to enemy clause.

---

[27]Ibid.; *Sadler's State Papers*, 1:175-7, Sadler to Henry 8, 1 May 1543.

[28]Ibid., p. 168-73; *Hamilton Papers*, 1:530-1, Sadler to Henry 8, 1 May 1543.

[29]Ibid,; *Sadler's State Papers*, 1:172-4, Sadler to Henry 8, 1 May 1543; *State Papers*, 5:284-5, Arran to Henry 8, 6 May 1543.

They would not, however, take part with France against Henry. The governor had argued before them without success that the Scots might as well "covenent" openly against France, as to promise to take no part with that nation for such unwillingness would undoubtedly offend its government. Hence, if either France or Denmark caused the Scots trouble, they would have to come on their knees to beseech Henry for assistance. Finally, regarding the negotiating of the treaty, Douglas and the pro-English Glencairn would be sent to confer with the English.[30]

On 6 May, Sadler wrote the privy council that it was impossible to do any more for the king's satisfaction. Apparently, there was now cause for optimism as Arran seemed more disposed towards Henry's will. Thus, Sadler could write that if the king did agree to the Scots' answer, he would be shortly able to do whatever he wanted in the northern kingdom. Ample time was of paramount importance. Not everything could be accomplished overnight. Sadler cautioned that a foundation must be laid before the complete edifice could be built.[31]

In response, the privy council directed Sadler to warn Arran of additional

---

[30]*Sadler's State Papers*, 1:170-1 and 183, Sadler to Henry 8, 1 May 1543; *Hamilton Papers*, 1:530-1, Sadler to Henry 8, 1 May 1543; Additional 32,650 folios 256-257, Arran to Henry 8, 4 May 1543; *Foedera, Conventiones, Literae, et Cujuscunque Generis Acta Publica, Inter Reges Angliae, et Alios Quosvis Imperatores, Reges, Pontifices, Principes, Vel Communitates, ab Ineunte Saeculo Duodecimo, viz. ab Anno 1101, ad nostra usque Tempora, Habita aut Tractata; Ex Autographis, infra Secretiores Archivorum Regiorum Thesaursrias, Per Multa Saecula Reconditis, Fideliter Escripta*. Edited by Thomas Rymer, 2nd ed. 20 vols. (London: J. Tonson, 1726-1735), 14:781. (Hereafter cited as *Foedera*.)

[31]*Sadler's State Papers*, 1:187, Sadler to the privy council, 6 May 1543; *Hamilton Papers*, 1:533, Sadler to the privy council, 6 May 1543.

dangers.[32]   On 25 March 1543, Pope Paul III had sent Mark Grimani, the patriarch of Aquileia, as the collector of a tribute of six-tenths which had been placed upon the Scots by the pontiff for their nation's defense. In addition, Grimani was to assist Cardinal Beaton in preserving Scotland from Henry's grasp. The French government was also involved in furthering this counter-reform diplomacy.[33]

Warnings of this mission, however, had little effect upon Arran. Henry's attempts to maneuver the governor by scare tactics were increasingly ineffective. Two communications from Arran in mid-May indicate that he was not as thoroughly inclined toward the Protestant camp as he had been. Perhaps the abbot's influence upon him accounted for some of this change. Letters written to both Pope Paul and the cardinal of Capri indicate a certain affinity with the Catholic cause. Arran explained to both men that he had been dilatory in sending ambassadors to Rome to salute the Holy See because of the stress of business which confronted him upon taking office for an infant sovereign in the midst of war with England. The English king's threat to the liberty of Scotland now, however, had forced the governor to show his devotion to Rome and to commit his kingdom to the protection of the pope.[34]

Arran also pointed out in this correspondence that the war with England had been caused by the refusal of Scotland to join Henry in a crusade against the authority of the pope. Thus, it was only right that the governor should ask

---

[32]*State Papers*, 5:285-8, the privy council to Sadler, 13 May 1543.

[33]*Letters and Papers*, vol. 18, pt. 1:181, Paul 3 to the governors of Scotland, 25 March 1543 and p. 226, Edmond Harvel to Henry 8, 8 April 1543.

[34]Royal Ms. 18 B VI folio 153b, Arran to Paul 3, 14 May 1543 and folio 154, Arran to the cardinal of Carpi, [sic] 14 May 1543.

Rome to assist him with money to defend the rights of his kingdom.[35]

Interestingly enough, Arran's correspondence with Pope Paul III came exactly twelve days after Beaton had written the papacy explaining why he was unable to attend the general council at Trent during Christmas. Even though the summons was late, had it arrived in time, the cardinal would not have been able to attend without great risk to his nation, owing to the tragedies surrounding James V's death and the English invasion. Beaton maintained that while he was defending the church's liberty and working to expel English impiety, he had been seized and placed in captivity for some three and one-half months. His incarceration was undeniably due to the instigation of Henry. The cardinal continued that even though he was still hated by his enemies, he was at least restored to the liberty he once knew. He concluded his letter to the pope by stating his willingness to strive as best he could for the church's safety.[36]

Such a rapprochement with Rome, especially on the part of the governor, was anathema to English interests. Above all, the king's party in the past could count at least on Arran's sympathy with religious reform along Henrician lines. But now, besides his wavering political loyalties, the governor showed a propensity to change faiths just as easily.

Hence, why should Arran not take "in marvellous good part" Henry's warning and advice concerning Grimani? If Francis I did no more harm than help send a papal legate to curse the Scots, the governor could care hardly at all. Grimani would bring upon himself his own destruction if he generated any "garboil" in the realm with his "fulminations" or sought to antagonize divisions

---

[35]Royal Ms. 18 B VI folio 154 only, Arran to cardinal.

[36]*Letters and Papers*, vol. 18, pt. 1:297-8, Cardinal Beaton to Paul 3, 1 May 1543.

within Scotland.[37]

Arran, characteristically stalling for time, offered Henry assistance in preventing the legate's coming on the condition that peace be established between their two realms. If peace were established, Arran, guided by Henry's recommendations, would quickly reduce the Scottish kingdom to obedience by reforming the church and advancing God's word. This would be done to satisfy the English king in spite of all the Catholics within Scotland.[38] Such was the governor's baffling behavior--all the more confusing as it was made only a few days after his plea to Rome. This duplicity once again shows that his policy was to keep Henry dangling by following a deliberate temporizing approach.

The governor's position was not an enviable one. The primary motive behind his policy was the earnest desire to avoid a resumption of hostilities which could threaten Scotland's cherished liberties as a sovereign nation. Hence, the governor stood between two major parties, each willing to resort to force. There were the ever-threatening Henry on the one hand and the Scottish clergy opposed to the threat of Protestant reforms on the other.

A large convocation of the Roman Catholic clergy had met in May at St. Andrews to determine how much money they would give to carry out a war with Henry should the need arise. They prorogued their assembly, however, until 1 June when the entire clergy was supposed to meet. Meanwhile, Sadler reported to the privy council on 20 May that a basic decision had been made to give all the money they had as well as their own plate and that of their churches

---

[37]*Sadler's State Papers*, 1:199-200, Sadler to the council, 20 May 1543; also in *Letters and Papers*, vol. 18, pt. 1:331-333.

[38]Ibid.; *Sadler's State Papers*, 1:200-1, Sadler to the council, 20 May 1543.

in the form of chalices, crosses, censers, and whatever else was necessary to combat the English party. The clergy were said to have gone so far as to say that they themselves were willing to fight if their services were needed.[39] Arran, once again displaying sympathy with the Protestant cause as well as stalling for time, asserted to the English party that if peace were established between the two British kingdoms, he would stop the clergy's assembly on 1 June.[40]

In a postscript to this correspondence, Sadler relayed news concerning Beaton. The cardinal had sent the governor a letter in which he acknowledged Henry's opposition to himself. So strong was the king's opposition that Beaton believed he stood as an obvious impediment to the unity of the two realms. In addition, in view of the fact that the cardinal had offered his services to Arran and they had been declined, he desired to move to France where he could still enjoy the benefits of his bishopric and any other revenues due him.[41]

Arran sought Sadler's advice on this request and was cautioned that such a move to France would be dangerous because the cardinal might freely work against the well-being of both their kingdoms. Hence, the governor affirmed that he would proceed against Beaton and his supporters according to Henry's counsel. Once again a condition was placed upon such action. Peace must be assured. Then, Arran would quickly snatch the prelate from what was described as his poorly fortified castle at St. Andrews.[42]

---

[39]Ibid., p. 204.

[40]Ibid.

[41]Ibid., pp. 206-7.

[42]Ibid., p. 207.

It may seem strange that both Henry and Sadler seemingly accepted Arran's repeated intentions to proceed against the pro-French-Catholic party if only the peace terms between the two kingdoms were ratified. But if Arran was not a faithful adherent to Henry's cause, who was left in a position of actual power in all of Scotland to carry out English policy? The king's assured lords were proving themselves to be more adept at taking English money than in furthering their master's designs. Therefore, the English had to take the alleged reformist governor at his word--there was no one else among the prominent Scottish personalities to rely upon. Arran now had the opportunity to test the English king's patience.

The Scottish governor's temporizing policy worked well. On 28 May he received word from Sadler that the truce between the two realms had been continued until 1 July. Arran had succeeded in avoiding war as the days of the campaign season slowly slipped by.[43]

Also during May, the English decided to return George Douglas to Scotland with instructions to obtain an agreement for the marriage of Mary and Edward based upon five specified conditions. The young queen was to be delivered to Henry or Edward at the age of eight or ten at most. Six earls and barons, or their heirs as approved by the king, plus two bishops, were to serve as hostages for her delivery at one of those times. In the meantime, she would remain in the custody of those Scottish nobles already appointed by parliament with the addition of two others. It was also maintained ". . . that for her education, instruction, saulf and holsome noriture, His Highnes may apoint and place such aboute her Person, Englisshe folke or other, as His Majeste shall

---

[43]Ibid., p. 209, Sadler to Arran, 28 May 1543; also in *Letters and Papers*, vol. 18, pt. 1:350.

thinke expedient." After Mary's delivery into England, her marriage would be solemnized by her twelfth year at most. Finally, when she became the queen of England she would be entitled to ". . . enyoye as grete a dower as moste commonly Quenes of this Realme have had and enyoyed."[44]

Regarding the so-called perpetual peace, it was to be like the last one with Scotland except that France was to be "pretermytted and lefte out." Part of Douglas's instructions concerned nations comprehended by Henry and the Scots. Should a nation detain or withhold either lands or pensions from either party, that nation would not receive the benefits of comprehension. No help nor favoritism would be shown such a nation. Neither would that nation be allowed to offer either party intelligence, nor would intercourse be allowed between them. In addition, both the English and the Scots could arrange to offer each other aid and assistance against any such nation. Wages or stipends were to be paid for such service.[45] Henry was intent upon rupturing "the auld alliance."

These new articles further stated that the hostages given for Mary's deliverance could also be bound for the observance of the peace until she was placed in Henry's hands.[46]

Douglas's list, however, did not fail to mention the future role of the key to English success--Arran. Henry was content that he continue in his role as governor until Mary's majority, provided that the treaties of marriage and peace were signed and he continued in his devotion to the king. Arran must also continue to use the council of those pro-English lords which he had followed in

---

[44]*State Papers*, 5:302-3, memorial for George Douglas, May 1543.

[45]Ibid., p. 303.

[46]Ibid.

the past. The governor would in return receive Henry's assistance against whoever threatened him. Finally, Arran was given free use of the Scottish treasury, with the exception of that part needed for the proper maintenance of the young queen.[47]

On 3 June Sadler reported that Arran was most willing to accept the new articles brought by Douglas. The governor, however, did not want to give the impression that he had agreed to them privately. Hence, he had summoned many of the Scottish nobles to Edinburgh to act upon them. Arran did not think that there would be much trouble in agreeing to all of the articles except the one concerning Mary's delivery at age ten. Nevertheless, he would do what he could in leading them into accepting even that provision. Angus, Cassillis, Somerville, and Douglas concurred with Arran's opinion concerning the articles' acceptance, adding that a large number of the Scottish lords acting upon them would add greater authority to the final conclusion. Finally, the governor stated that he had delayed the convocation of the clergy which had been prorogued until June. Once again, Arran asserted that if sure of peace, he would prosecute Beaton.[48]

When the Scottish nobles did convene, the anticipated objections were made to the queen's delivery at the age of ten.[49] On 8 June, however, the parliament of Scotland meeting at Edinburgh answered the articles brought by Douglas from Henry. Mary would be delivered to either the king or the prince

---

[47]Ibid., pp. 303-4.

[48]*Sadler's State Papers*, 1:209-11, Sadler to Suffolk and Parr, 3 June 1543; *Hamilton Papers*, 1:534-5, Sadler to Suffolk and Parr, 3 June 1543.

[49]Ibid., p. 535, Sadler to Henry 8, 7 June 1543; *Sadler's State Papers*, 1:212, Sadler to Henry 8, 7 June 1543.

at ten years of age provided that the marriage would be made by proxy when she left the kingdom. Six earls or barons and their heirs would serve as hostages or pledges of the Scots' sincerity. Every six months they would be changed. For the time being, the lords named in parliament were to maintain custody of the young queen. Henry, however, could send a man of worship from his nation as well as a lady accompanied by a retinue of not more than twenty people which would attend the Scottish sovereign at his expense.

Since Mary was the queen of Scotland, the parliament thought that her dowry should be specified in the marriage contract. Concerning the actual peace between the two countries, the English article was slightly altered to protect the intercourse of Scottish merchants. The Scots also maintained that no prisoners should be held in either kingdom as gentleness and love should always be shown between the two realms. Scottish prisoners detained by the English were to be ransomed. In addition, should Edward die before Mary and without heirs, the Scottish queen should be able, if she chose, to return home to her native land free from the bonds of any marriage.

Concerning Arran, the parliament held that at Mary's "perfect age" and deliverance into England, she, Henry, and Edward must not hold him accountable for his handling of Scottish revenues. In conclusion, the Scots would be able to enjoy their traditional liberties, governed by one from their own realm and under their own laws.[50]

An agreement with Henry seemed nearly at hand. Yet, this reply of the Scottish parliament plainly indicated that nationalism was still alive in that

---

[50]Ibid., pp. 212-15; *Hamilton Papers*, 1:535, Sadler to Henry 8, 7 June 1543; Additional 32,651 folios 7 and 9 and Sloane 3199 folio 232 for Arran's answer to the marriage proposal of 1543 between Edward and Mary, 8 June 1543.

kingdom. Henry's initial demands had been greatly altered because of Scottish pride and perseverance.

Moray, Huntly, and Argyle, the conservative lords who had served with Arran on Beaton's short-lived regency council, were not present at the parliament which formulated this reply to Douglas's memorial. Moray was sick; Huntly was occupied in the north; and Argyle was subduing an insurrection against himself in the Highlands. The governor, nonetheless, was pleased that these men were not able to attend. In particular, he was glad that Moray and Huntly were not there because they would have made it more difficult to agree to the English proposals.

Sadler reported to Henry that Arran had seemed completely dedicated to the English cause in gaining support for the articles. The king had also been aided by Angus, Cassillis, Somerville, and George Douglas, who with great difficulty worked to secure the treaties' acceptance by parliament. Douglas, greatly trusted and appreciated by the governor, was to leave soon for England with the Scots' answer.[51]

Despite the fact that the Scots and the English were coming closer to an understanding, some of Henry's advisors continued to distrust Arran. Sadler, nonetheless, ardently defended the governor:

> ... If he be a Christian man, and have any spot of honour, honesty, or truth in him, he is wholly dedicate to the king's majesty, and the most desirous man that ever I saw, in appearance, to have the king's majesty his good and gracious

---

[51]*Sadler's State Papers*, 1:212-15, Sadler to Henry 8, 7 June 1543; *Hamilton Papers*, 1:535, Sadler to Henry 8, 7 June 1543; Additional 32,651 folio 12, Arran to Lisle, 8 June 1543.

lord.[52]

The English ambassador seemed certain of the governor's sincerity as he relayed a common opinion of him to some of the king's more skeptical followers: Arran was not only a heretic, but a good Englishman who had sold Scotland to the English as well. Sadler also added that the governor had to be a good Englishman since his ancestors were from the southern kingdom.[53] Such reasoning was typical of Henry's whole Scottish policy in 1543.

In June, Arran became extremely ill and was confined at his home in Hamilton some thirty miles from Edinburgh. This illness kept Sadler from following what had become his usual approach of dealing with the governor. Specifically this involved urging Arran to keep his promises and above all to move swiftly against Beaton and his party since the long-sought peace between the two kingdoms was nearly at hand. But as summer drew near, even Sadler discerned that the governor had begun to ". . . waxeth somewhat cold" when this subject was once again raised.[54]

By early summer, Henry's secret purpose to subvert Scottish sovereignty had become generally known. This recognition went far towards accounting for Arran's continuing vacillation as he realized that he was merely being used as Henry's catspaw. Sadler's incessant warnings of the French party were in part

---

[52]*Sadler's State Papers*, 1:215-16, Sadler to Suffolk and Parr, 9 June 1543; *Hamilton Papers*, 1:538-9, Sadler to Suffolk and Parr, 9 June 1543.

[53]Ibid.

[54]Additional 32,651 folio 33, Arran to Sadler, 19 June 1543; *Hamilton Papers*, 1:545, Sadler to Suffolk and Parr, 19 June 1543 and p. 546, enclosure by the governor in Sadler to the privy council, 19 June 1543; *Sadler's State Papers*, 1:219-30, Sadler to Suffolk and Parr, 19 June 1543.

a facade to conceal the identity of Scotland's real enemy.[55] The irony of this remarkable episode in Anglo-Scottish relations is that the politically inexperienced governor perceived more clearly that actual situation than did Henry's experienced chief representative. The king's policy would soon suffer, in no small measure because of Sadler's lack of perception.

By the end of June Arran had recuperated enough to return to the Scottish capital where the ambassador resumed his futile approach. What Sadler once again found was a seemingly well-minded but hesitant governor. Arran seemed convinced that the English could help him much more than the French could ever hope to assist his opponents. Yet, the governor would follow Henry's advice concerning the cardinal and Lennox as well as in ". . . all other thinges tending to the common wealthe and benefite of this realme," only when the peace was finally concluded and now, the pledges "layed." Arran maintained that acting before the treaties were finalized might jeopardize his chances of gathering pledges and would hence harm the security of the peace.[56]

As the terms of peace neared ratification, the governor grew uneasy seeking a new excuse to delay action upon these English recommendations and to prolong his play for time. Therefore Arran decided to fall back on the issue of securing pledges, which in fact proved to be a serious problem.

Even the news of the arrival of a French fleet off Aberdeen with money, munitions, and messages for the queen dowager, Beaton, and Lennox, did not lead Arran to follow Sadler's advice in moving the teething queen from Linlithgow to Edinburgh. The governor was not bothered by the fleet's

---

[55] *Hamilton Papers*, 1:li.

[56] Ibid., pp. 548-9, Sadler to the privy council, 29 June 1543.

presence; he only had fear of French gold. Arran calmly assured the ambassador that he would provide for the young queen's safety against whatever French designs there were. So convincing was Arran concerning Mary's safety that Sadler remarked that he treated her as if she were his own child.[57]

Sadler's extreme faith in and defense of the Scottish governor, in spite of Arran's hesitation to do as he was advised, stood in sharp contrast to the more perceptive and skeptical attitudes of other adherents of the king's party. Parr had gained the information that everything which the Scottish governor had promised to Henry was merely "craft, frawde, and falsitie." According to Parr, Arran neither intended nor was able to keep his promises. In view of efforts to get the Scots to agree to their queen's delivery to Henry at ten years of age, Parr's informant reported that Arran had argued before his council:

> . . . Ye knowe the king of Englande is a mightie prince and we not able nez of powre to resist his puissance, and for that cause I thinke and take it best by fare wordes and promyses, with the concluding of this peas, to deferre and put over the danger that might otherwise fall upon us and in the meane tyme the yong Quene maye chance to die or other change maye happene, wherebie Scotlande maye bee relieved and more able to resist Englande.[58]

The queen dowager had clearly perceived the situation months earlier. Like so many others, however, she was unsuccessful in sharpening Sadler's perception.

---

[57]Ibid., p. 550, Sadler to the privy council, 30 June 1543 and p. 551, Sadler to the privy council, 2 July 1543; *Sadler's State Papers*, 1:225-6, Sadler to the privy council, 30 June 1543 and pp. 226-8, Sadler to the privy council, 2 July 1543.

[58]Additional 32, 651 folio 55-55v., Lord Parr to the duke of Suffolk, 6 July 1543.

Arran had explained the logic behind his desire to temporize with the English. He indicated that he was up to his own game of deceit, intending to extend the peace for as long as he could, or until, at least, Scotland was in a better position to deal with its grasping neighbor to the south. The governor of Scotland was wiser than many of his contemporaries gave him credit for being. Arran's vacillation was deliberately intended to wreck Henry's designs upon Scotland. The governor's play for time succeeded inasmuch as French interests waxed while those of the English waned. Many Scotsmen, however, failed to see the soundness of Arran's approach.

In July, English intelligence reported that the governor's only assured followers regarding the treaty were Angus, Cassillis, Maxwell, and their own particular adherents. "All the rest of Scotlande, both spirituell and temporall" opposed Arran. Negative opinions of the governor continued to circulate. He was said to be very poor, having spent that which was given to him by the king as well as that gathered on his own in hopes of winning friends to his cause. Seemingly, no one feared the governor as he was ". . . of small witte or pollicie to compasse, conduce, or bring to effecte a matier of any ymportance, and lesse able and constante to perfourme that which he promysethe." [59] With such accounts originating in Arran's native Scotland, little wonder that shortly after James V's death and during the early days of his regency, continental reports described him as part idiot, "half-witted," or "*a demy folz et insense*," quite unfit to wear the crown of his kingdom. [60]

---

[59]Ibid.

[60]Great Britain, Public Record Office, *Calendar of Letters, Despatches, and State Papers, Relating to Negotiations between England and Spain Preserved in the Archives at Simancas and Elsewhere*, edited by Royall Tyler et al., 13 vols. (London: Her Majesty's Stationery Office,

Such were the contemporary accounts of the man leading the nation with which Henry VIII entrusted the treaties of marriage and peace on 1 July 1543 at Greenwich, England.[61]

With the Scottish question seemingly behind him, the English king could devote more careful attention to his major concern on the continent--namely the war which he and his ally, the Holy Roman Emperor and king of Spain, Charles V, were waging against Francis I. But unfortunately for England, its backdoor was not firmly secured. The governor of Scotland held its key--not Henry.

1862-1954), vol. 6, pt. 2, 28 December 1542, Chapuys to the queen of Hungary, p. 192, and 15 January 1543, Chapuys to Charles 5, pp. 223 and 228. (Hereafter cited as *Spanish Calendar*.)

[61]Additional 32,651 folio 51, Henry 8 to Arran, 3 July 1543; *Foedera*, 14:786-797; *Letters and Papers*, vol. 18, pt. 1:454-8, treaties with Scotland and the ransom of Scottish prisoners, 1 July 1543.

CHAPTER V

The Solidification of Sentiments:
The Scottish Reaction to the Treaties of Greenwich

After Henry had finally given his approval to the treaties, he was anxious
for the Scots to ratify them as soon as possible. The English king was well
aware that his neighbor's government to the north remained in a state of
disarray. Sensing an opportunity to enhance his position, he sought to enlarge
Arran's council with a new group of his own supporters. The king had also
drawn up a set of secret articles for his assured lords to follow should confusion
lead either to the death or removal of the young queen, or to the death or revolt
of Arran. Three of the five Scottish ambassadors--Douglas, Glencairn, and
Learmouth--knew these plans. Hamilton and Balnavis, however, were not
informed of them as the English did not believe that they were as well disposed
as the other three.[1]

At the same time, Henry appointed Sadler and his wife to reside with the
young Mary. On 13 July, however, Sadler earnestly begged his king to retract
this appointment. The ambassador believed that his wife was "most unmeet" for

---

[1]*Hamilton Papers*, 1:559-60, Henry 8 to Sadler, 7 July 1543.

the job. She suffered from a lack of courtly training as well as being pregnant.[2] Lady Sadler's unsuitability as a royal attendant stemmed from the fact that she had once been a laundress in the household of Thomas Cromwell, her husband's patron. She had also married the ambassador when her first husband, Matthew Barre, a tradesman from London, was still living. In fact, only in December 1554 were Sadler's eight children by her legitimized.[3]

Such conduct on the part of Henry VIII was characteristic of English policy in regard to Scotland following his success at Solway Moss. This inept diplomacy even led to an assassination attempt upon Sadler as he walked in his Edinburgh garden in mid-July.[4] Instead of helping to pacify relations between the two nations, Henry's ambassador inevitably became the target of the rising indignation of the anti-English party.

The prospects of a ratification of the treaties clearly led to a closing of ranks in both the cardinal's and the governor's parties. Arran had called a convention in Edinburgh for the purpose of ratification. This convention, however, was rivalled by one summoned by Beaton's followers to meet at Stirling on 20 July. Among those furthering the cardinal's assembly were Huntly, Argyle, Lennox, and Bothwell. They also intended to make raids into England in order to break the peace. The primary purpose behind Beaton's designs, so Arran believed, was to march to Linlithgow to gain possession of the young queen and thereby put his government down. Henry's dire warnings

---

[2]Ibid., pp. 569-70, Sadler to Henry 8, 13 July 1543; *Sadler's State Papers*, 1:229-30, Sadler to Henry 8, 13 July 1543.

[3]*Hamilton Papers*, 1:lii.

[4]Ibid., p. 573, Sadler to Henry 8, 17 July 1543; *Sadler's State Papers*, 1:236-7, Sadler to Henry 8, 17 July 1543.

were seemingly on the verge of becoming truth as the cardinal's party increasingly gained strength.

Although concerned about this development, Arran felt capable of handling himself well as he boasted to Sadler that within a few days, he would have some twenty thousand men who would not desist until he had gotten his revenge on the prelate and his followers. The governor's opposition acted on the pretense of defending their faith and church as well as the liberty of Scotland. To this group, Arran was just as Sadler reported--a heretic and a good Englishman. The governor was confident that Henry would come to his aid. The king's assistance was to be in the form of money, which could be given in good faith for Arran ". . . would spend his life to keep all his promises" to Henry. The governor, however, hesitated to receive English forces as he already had enough men--provided that the French did not seek to re-enforce Beaton's band. On 17 July, Arran planned to go to Linlithgow where his men would assemble. Should his opposition come forward, he would take the queen to the impregnable fortress of Blackness. Afterwards, he would move his forces on to Stirling where he intended to meet his adversaries in the field.[5]

The English king continued to press his treaties upon the Scots in spite of such national sentiment against them. Henry wrote to Sadler stating his satisfaction with Arran's conduct and forwarding to the governor one thousand pounds with hints of further support in cash should he prove himself worthy and needful. Among other matters, the governor was to be advised by Sadler to proclaim Beaton and his party as traitors. He was to remove Mary to Tantallon

---

[5]Additional 32, 651, folio 110, Arran to Glencairn and Douglas, 16 July 1543; *Sadler's State Papers*, 1:233-5, Sadler to Henry 8, 16 July 1543; *Hamilton Papers*, 1:572-3 Sadler to Henry 8, 16 July 1543.

and above all to seclude her from her mother. Arran had also to see that the Scottish strongholds were placed in sure hands. Additional advice would be given him on how to progress should a military confrontation between his and the cardinal's forces ensue.[6]

In spite of Arran's apparent belief that he had enough forces to deal with the cardinal, the skeptical Parr had been informed to the contrary:

> . . . the governour is no parte like in strenthe to the cardinall parte, for he is not past x thousande men, and the other side is takene to bee xxx thousande; and he [Parr's informant] saithe there is no other waye for the governour but either to feight, orelles to be induced to the contrarie parte, whiche he thinkethe he woll rather doo thene feght.[7]

On 22 July, Sadler reported to his king that the two parties were coming to a showdown at Linlithgow. The governor, who had been assured that he would be furnished both English recruits and money if necessary, had garrisoned the queen's fortress with enough men and munitions to protect her from Beaton's followers, now estimated to number no more than six or seven thousand. Arran's forces, numbering around seven to eight thousand, were preparing for the confrontation, where they were to compose their differences either peacefully or by force.[8]

On 24 July Beaton and his party did gather at Linlithgow for the purpose

---

[6]Ibid., p. 587, Henry 8 to Sadler, 22 July 1543; *Sadler's State Papers*, 1:238-41, Henry 8, to Sadler, 22 July 1543.

[7]*Hamilton Papers*, 1:582-3, Parr to Suffolk, 22 July 1543.

[8]Ibid., pp. 584-5, Sadler to Henry 8, 22 July 1543.

of signing a secret bond. The document provided for a mutual defense against the political maneuvers of Arran, and was intended to prevent Mary and the queen dowager from being taken into Henry VIII's possession.[9]

Fortunately, a military confrontation between the cardinal's and the governor's parties was avoided. On the same day as the bond was formed, Sadler reported that an agreement between the two factions was at hand. Hence, the money which Arran had earlier requested was not needed at that time. Sadler, therefore, decided to keep the one thousand pounds until it could be more fruitfully bestowed to achieve his king's purpose.[10]

Negotiations took place between the two factions six miles outside of Edinburgh--midway between the capital city and Linlithgow. Beaton's followers requested that Arran's government recognize four petitions. First, Mary should be taken from the custody of the governor and placed under the protection of those Scottish lords named by parliament. Second, a new council should be appointed to advise Arran. Third, should the governor not heed that counsel and continue to follow the private advice of others, he should resign his office. Fourth, the Douglases should not visit the Scottish court until Beaton and the leading earls supporting the cardinal had met with the governor and determined these matters. Glencairn reported that Arran had granted the first two petitions and denied the others.[11]

Two days later, on 26 July, Sadler wrote to his king describing three

---

[9]Sloane 3199 folio 247, Cardinal of St. Andrews and other nobles versus Arran and his party, 24 July 1543.

[10]*Hamilton Papers*, 1:589-90, Sadler to Suffolk and Tunstall, 24 July 1543.

[11]Ibid.

areas of agreement between the Arran and Beaton camps. First, Mary would be taken from the governor and placed in the custody of four Scottish barons appointed by parliament. Second, within a short time, a day and a place were to be appointed where Arran could have an honorable and quiet meeting with the nobility of both parties for the ratification of the treaties and for the establishment of his advisory council. The third area involved Beaton and his supporters meeting with Angus and the governor's supporters in an effort to display their sincerity concerning the points of agreement.

On 25 July this gathering between the two rival factions took place. Sadler reported:

> . . . there was shakyng of handes oone with an other, freendlie embrasinges and famyliar communications, and verie good agreament amongst them, and long and familier talke betwixt therle of Anguysshe and the cardinal, so that it is thought that good friendship wooll ensue on all partes.[12]

As a result of this meeting, the lords--"Graym, Erskyn, Lyndesey, and Leveniton"--approved by parliament were named as the queen's custodians. Two were chosen by Arran, and two by Beaton. Each of the men was to be accorded equal rights within Linlithgow Castle. Glencairn asserted that they would keep the young queen and deliver her as specified in the treaty. As a result of this bargain, he also held that the Scottish nobles would be more willing to remain in England as pledges of their nation's good faith. Allaying English fears, Beaton openly said that contrary to popular opinion, his party wanted it to be known that they were dedicated to the treaties of peace and

---

[12]Ibid., pp. 592-3, Sadler to Henry 8, 26 July 1543.

marriage, and were as proud of them as anyone within Scotland. With such unanimity of opinion, it was generally agreed that the peace should be proclaimed in Edinburgh and on the borders.[13]

The peace was celebrated with great fanfare within the Scottish capital. Heralds and trumpeters signalled the jubilation greeting this agreement with the English as Arran and his supporters lined the High Street in Edinburgh. This was perhaps the governor's most triumphant day as regent of Scotland. Not only had he and the English king come to terms, but an apparent conciliation with his Scottish opposition had just occurred.[14]

The two rival factions within Scotland were seemingly beginning to work together. With the common consent of both groups, the young queen and her mother were transferred from Linlithgow to Stirling. The former home was so small that Mary's four new custodians could not be comfortably lodged.[15] On 28 July, a satisfied Arran wrote to Henry thanking him for his advice and support in quelling this so-called insurrection.[16]

On the same day that Arran expressed this gratitude, however, the usually confident Sadler seemed apprehensive about the Scottish situation as he wrote, ". . . so moche, untrewthe, jalousie, feare, and suspicion," existed between the men there that he did not know what to believe.[17] The ambassador's

---

[13]Ibid.

[14]Ibid., p. 597.

[15]Ibid.

[16]Additional 32,651 folios 157-58, Arran to Henry 8, 28 July 1543.

[17]*Hamilton Papers*, 1:602, Sadler to Henry 8, 28 July 1543.

perception of Scottish affairs had begun to sharpen.

There were indications that the cardinal's party would insist that the coming parliamentary convention meet at Stirling. The fact that the young queen had already been moved there was enough for Arran. He, therefore, insisted that his base of operation--Edinburgh, not Stirling--should be where the assembly convened. To show his displeasure Arran remarked that he had rather travel to London without a safe-conduct than to go to Stirling.

The alleged offer of the cardinal's group that they would both serve and obey the governor and even show their sincerity by contracting a marriage between his son and the queen who would be committed to his sole protection, failed to move Arran. His rejection of this offer was due to the fact that he along with the three estates of Scotland had already come to an agreement with Henry concerning the treaties of peace and marriage. The governor, acting in stark contrast to popular opinion of him, gave the impression of being a man of his word, perpetually loyal to the English king, as he declined the suggestion that he leave his southern neighbor by joining Beaton's party.[18] If such were the case, the cardinal's faction certainly could not be trusted by the English.

In view of this suspicion cast upon Beaton by the governor, other adherents of the king, with the exception of Douglas, refused to believe that the cardinal's followers were now opposed to the treaties. According to them, Arran had fabricated the story in order to enhance his position with Henry.[19]

Douglas, still chief among the governor's counsellors, maintained that Arran was of a good mind and determination towards Henry, although Beaton's

---

[18]Ibid., p. 603.

[19]Ibid., pp. 605-6.

party, in spite of their words, was adverse to him. Thus, the thousand pounds should be given to the governor as he was without money. Should this need go unnoticed, Arran would be forced into minting some. According to Douglas, one thousand pounds would be of greater benefit to the governor then than three thousand would be later. Sadler concurred with this opinion.[20]

The English ambassador concluded his lengthy report to his king by writing that Arran had made a very significant comment concerning his loyalty to the English cause should Beaton and his followers not support the Greenwich treaties and should they deprive him of office so that he could not keep his own treaty commitments. Facing such a situation, the governor would place all the major strongholds south of the Firth of Forth under English control. Hence, the king would command such a powerful position within Scotland that his will would certainly be done.[21]

Henry was satisfied with this generous offer. He gave Sadler permission to give Arran the one thousand pounds--a mere token of what the English king would bestow upon this humble servant should he be more responsive to Henry's interests.[22]

The king commanded Sadler to caution the governor of Beaton's true motives. Specifically, the prelate should not be allowed on Arran's advisory council unless he renounced his "red hode" and agreed that ". . . Goddes Word may be set furthe according to the governours determynacion."[23]

---

[20]Ibid., pp. 606 and 608.

[21]Ibid., p. 609.

[22]Ibid., pp. 616-7, the privy council to Sadler, 2 August 1543.

[23]Ibid., p. 611, Henry 8 to Sadler, 31 July 1543.

There was basis for the king's hesitation in accepting Beaton's sincerity. At the same time as Henry expressed his distrust of the cardinal, Sadler wrote to his king that the prelate was once again plotting against the governor.[24]

Within a few days of this warning, Henry ordered Sadler to declare to Arran and others of his party that they had been both abused and deceived by the cardinal.[25] Seemingly sincere expressions of goodwill on the part of both parties given only a few days earlier had quickly dissipated. The realm of Scottish politics was a difficult one to fathom.

A military force of five thousand men, or even a greater one if necessary, could be sent by the king to insure Arran's success against the prelate. Henry's advice, however, would have to be followed by the governor. Beaton had to be captured or at least driven over the Forth. All Scottish strongholds in the south must also be delivered. But as if Henry had not already been generous enough, should the cardinal's party capture the queen and renounce the English marriage, the king would by force of his title and superiority make Arran the king of Scotland north of the Forth. The governor would still be expected to follow through with the marriage of his son and the English princess.[26] What more could Arran expect?

Arran, however, was not Henry's fool, especially when his desired conduct would involve outright treason. He revealed his lack of enthusiasm about the king's offer to make him king of the north by simply replying that all

---

[24]Ibid., p. 612, Sadler to Henry 8, 31 July 1543; *Sadler's State Papers*, 1:242-5, Sadler to Henry 8, 31 July 1543.

[25]*Hamilton Papers*, 1:618, to Sadler, 3 August 1543.

[26]Ibid., p. 620, Henry 8 to Sadler, 4 August 1543; *Sadler's State Papers*, 1:246-49, Henry 8 to Sadler, 4 August 1543.

of his lands lay on the southern side of the Forth. The governor was not interested. Such a stance does much to discredit the opinions of those who held that the governor was little more than an inconstant simpleton. Even Henry's offer of five thousand troops was declined. Arran gave his thanks but replied that the aid of five thousand Englishmen would make twenty thousand Scots forsake them.

Arran, however, suggested that Henry's recruits might be kept in readiness should the situation be drastically altered. Despite having offended the king by this refusal, the governor proceeded to request that Henry lend him five thousand pounds within ten days which would allow him to gain the help of enough of his native Scotsmen to bring Beaton and his followers into line with English desires. He had just spent twenty thousand "merks Scots" in the latest "ruffle." Therefore, Henry would see why five thousand men were of less use to him than five thousand pounds.[27]

The English king was not so understanding. Such actions on the part of Arran did not please Henry. He did not see how such a loan could be used to his benefit. Beaton was ". . . so rooted towardes Fraunce in affection" that he could never be altered unless he was ". . . plucked up by the rootes"--captured or driven out of the realm. How many times had the English suggested the capture of Beaton to the governor, all to no avail? What did Arran plan to do now that the cardinal had pledged to support the treaties of peace and marriage? Had perhaps the tables begun to turn? Now that the governor was giving the appearance of believing what Sadler had warned him all along, Henry backed off with his money. If five thousand English troops were not good enough for

---

[27]Ibid., pp. 253-58, Sadler to Henry 8, 10 August 1543; *Hamilton Papers*, 1:629-30, Sadler to Henry 8, 9 August 1543.

Arran, then neither was a loan of five thousand pounds.

Perhaps the English king was trying to play the two rival Scottish factions against each other, hoping thereby to achieve his own purposes more quickly. Regardless, Henry maintained that Arran and his friends in Scotland could easily uproot the cardinal and his faction if they would go immediately to work. Beaton's party, so the king held, could not stand up to the governor's. France was not able to assist the cardinal as it should. Matters at home had preoccupied the French king's attention. The English navy, moreover, was in a position to take care of whatever French intervention there should be. As Henry's designs on Scotland grew nearer fruition by a ratification of the treaties, the more confident he became of Arran's strength in relation to that of the cardinal.[28]

Earlier in the month of August, the governor had expressed apprehension concerning the feasibility of convening parliament to ratify the treaties on the date set, the twentieth. Beaton's party feared for its safety in Edinburgh, as Arran did for his in Stirling. In spite of this controversy, the cardinal's group had finally agreed to all the articles and to their formal ratification taking place in the capital city. A major problem, however, was that the date set for it was entirely too early. Although the treaties with England required ratification within two months after Henry approved them in July, a truly representative parliament would have trouble convening by then. Arran requested that Henry postpone the ratification date and the giving of hostages until 30 September so that Beaton's faction might be present to lend greater authority to the treaties. If Henry did not consent to this request, then Arran would ratify the treaties

---

[28]Ibid., pp. 637-8, Henry 8 to Sadler, 16 August 1543.

without waiting for Beaton and his supporters.[29]

Henry, however, refused to grant a delay for the treaties' ratification as it would ". . . sumwhat losen and set at libertie the strenght of the bargayn concluded" by the five commissioners sent by the Scottish parliament to negotiate in London. According to the king, since the cardinal's party had already agreed to the treaties, Arran alone had the power to ratify them in the name and with the consent of the three estates of parliament. For Henry, another formal parliament was completely unnecessary. The Scottish parliament had in effect already given its approval by sending the ambassadors with a definite commission to negotiate with him. "The presence of this or that particular person in passing of the same" was now unimportant to Henry.[30] The sooner the governor formally ratified the Greenwich treaties the better. But ratification or not, Henry, one way or another, would do his best to gain possession of the young queen of Scotland.

Henry's dissatisfaction with the Scots mounted. He even instructed Sadler to circumvent the articles of the treaty and to do what he could to enlarge the number of his supporters around Mary at Stirling. The ambassador was to handle this matter secretly with Arran and others sympathetic to his interests as if it were an indifferent concern.[31]

Henry gave further instructions to his ambassador. Mary of Guise was not to be permitted to remain in the same castle with her daughter. Rather, she along with two or three accompanying her, were to be accorded the liberty to

---

[29]Ibid., pp. 622-4, Sadler to Henry 8, 5 August 1543.

[30]Ibid., p. 628, the privy council to Sadler, 9 August 1543.

[31]Ibid., lv-lvi and 633-4, Henry 8 to Sadler, 10 August 1543.

visit the queen only occasionally.[32]

When the governor was approached with these ideas, he maintained that he had no personal objection to enlarging the number of Englishmen, but parliament had already set the number. Of even greater importance, however, was the fact that Mary of Guise could not be moved from Stirling Castle as it was her own house, part of her jointure.[33]

The queen dowager represented a major threat to the king's designs. Her repeated assertions of loyalty to Sadler concerning her desire to further Henry's cause failed to convince the skeptical king. In August, she sent for the English ambassador to meet with her at Stirling. She was still desirous of the marriage and was more optimistic about its fruition now that her daughter had been taken out of the hands of the governor and placed in those of the men chosen by parliament. Defending Beaton's recent intentions, the dowager held that Arran had been keeping her and the young queen in virtual prison on the basis that she was attempting to remove the lass from Scotland. Once again, Sadler was confronted with a barrage of words aimed at undermining the position of the one person whom he considered a faithful adherent to his king.[34]

This interview, coupled with one Douglas had with the cardinal, seemed to suggest that the English king would indeed have his way concerning the treaties of peace and marriage. In a discussion with Douglas, whom he had summoned to St. Andrews, Beaton stated his desire for Douglas to do what he

---

[32]Ibid., 633.

[33]Ibid., pp. 642-3, Sadler to Henry 8, 17 August 1543.

[34]Ibid., pp. 629-30, Sadler to Henry 8, 9 August 1543; *Sadler's State Papers*, 1:249-53, Sadler to Henry 8, 10 August 1543.

could to help bring the cardinal into Henry's and Arran's favor. Thereby, he would be able to serve both British realms. If Douglas found this to be impossible, the cardinal should at least be given permission to live quietly outside of Scotland. Such a request, as already noted, had been made to the governor and denied upon Sadler's advice.

The cardinal, nevertheless, was persistent in his discussion. He described in vivid terms to Douglas the dread and perplexity in which he lived. Many of the Scottish nobles had wronged him--getting from him almost all he had. Beaton's trust and confidence in the Scots seemed as meager as that of the English. Also in this conference, Douglas touched upon the confrontation which had just occurred between his and Arran's parties. Beaton maintained that it was staged primarily to secure the welfare of the church from the governor's reformist tendencies.

Douglas proposed that if the cardinal would become a true servant of Arran, Henry would pardon his past actions and show him favor. Beaton replied that he had been misconstrued in the past and had never offended the English monarch. He was prepared to ". . . settfourthe and accomplishe all thinges to your majestes contentacion, and the common weale of the realme." Yet, when Douglas recommended that he be present at Edinburgh with the governor for the ratification of the treaties, Beaton excused himself by arguing that he had promised the nobles of his party not to go to Arran unless they gave him their consent. In particular, the cardinal feared the governor's lightness and inconstancy as well as the malice of his wife who Beaton knew "loved him not."

The prelate requested that the governor be allowed to handle the concerns with England even though he and his followers might not be there. Afterwards, they would have the time to pacify whatever arguments still existed between them. Even though the military forces for both sides should remain intact, Beaton left Douglas with the promise that he would try to get his followers' permission to meet with Arran in Edinburgh or to get the governor to meet with him at St. Andrews.[35]

From all appearances, it seemed that the king's business was progressing reasonably well. At least there were verbal assurances from all the major personalities that the treaties of peace and marriage would be shortly ratified with their approval, one way or another. Little did Henry know that as the day of the treaties' ratification neared, so too did his Scottish policy edge toward total disaster.

---

[35]*Hamilton Papers*, 1:639-41, Sadler to Henry 8, 17 August 1543.

CHAPTER VI

The Defection of Arran
and the Crumbling of English Policy

On 25 August, Henry VIII's cherished dream of many months came true. At the abbey of Holyrood House, in the presence of the greater part of the Scottish nobility, Arran ratified the treaties of peace and marriage with the English in the name of the queen and the three estates of parliament. The Great Seals of both nations were exchanged in the ceremony. Not surprisingly, however, Beaton and his band of followers were not present.[1]

John Knox pointed out in his description of that event:

> . . . and that nothing should lack that might fortify the matter, was Christ's body sacred (as Papists term it), broken betwix the said Governor and Master Sadler, Ambassador, and received of them both as a sign and token of the unity of their minds, inviolably to keep that contract, in all points, as they looked of Christ Jesus to be saved, and after to be reputed men worthy of

---

[1]Additional 32,651 folios 277-80, two letters from Arran to Henry 8, 25 August 1543; *Sadler's State Papers*, 1:270-1, Sadler to Henry 8, 25 August 1543; *Hamilton Papers*, 1:655-6, Sadler to Henry 8, 25 August 1543.

credit before the world.[2]

The symbolism of this Roman communion was more profound than the English suspected.[3] The reformist governor had truly begun to lose some of his zeal in regard to Henry's plans. The reasons are not hard to discern.

The absence of the cardinal and his party at the ratification ceremony frustrated Arran. The next day, following Beaton's suggestion to Douglas, the governor arrived in St. Andrews for the purpose of composing differences which existed with the prelate. To Arran's indignation, the cardinal did not show him the slightest amount of respect. Beaton would not move--refusing to come out of his castle to meet or to speak with the governor. Thoroughly humiliated, Arran declared that the cardinal was guilty of treason and returned to the capital city shortly thereafter.[4]

A military confrontation between the two parties was once again a strong possibility. Some within the king's party urged Henry to support Arran either with money or by sending an army strong enough to conquer the kingdom. The governor, apparently sensing his nadir--only days after his triumphant rejoicing along the High Street in Edinburgh--stated that he would have to adhere to the English king for he had lost all of his other friends and was in tremendous

---

[2]Knox, *History*, 1:46-7.

[3]Slavin, *Politics and Profit*, p. 126.

[4]Additional 32,651 folio 281, Arran to Henry 8, August 1543; *Hamilton Papers*, 1:664-5, Sadler to Henry 8, 29 August 1543; *Sadler's State Papers*, 1:277-82, Sadler to Henry 8, 28 August 1543; Annie Isabella Cameron, ed., *The Scottish Correspondence of Mary of Lorraine: Including Some Three Hundred Letters from 20th February 1542-1543 to 15th May 1560*, Scottish History Society Publications, third series, vol. 10 (Edinburgh: University Press, 1927), pp. 26-7, communication by Methven, 27 August 1543. (Hereafter cited as *Scottish Correspondence*.)

danger. But Arran could not even secure any word on an extension of the expiring peace with his supposed friend and neighbor.[5]

The intent to follow Henry, however, just like so many other statements made to the English in the past, was not kept by the governor. Pressures upon Arran were entirely too great. He began to scramble for ways to back down in fulfilling his promises to the English king. His pledge to deliver all the major strongholds south of the Forth to Henry should the treaties not be fulfilled, was explained away by the fact that he meant something quite different. These fortresses would be placed in the hands of only those men, such as himself, who were ready to serve the English king.[6] A big difference existed between Arran and Henry. One man was certainly not the other.

Finally, the governor discovered that he would have to disassociate himself completely from the English king, as Henry's bold actions had left him with little alternative. The people of Edinburgh were not blind to the situation. Both men and women, especially the merchants, were so enraged with the English party that Sadler and his house were even in danger of being burned. Concerning Arran, he had "coloured a peax" meant only to undo the Scots. Little wonder the governor had no more friends.[7]

The action of the English king to which the citizens of Edinburgh objected most was the seizure of five or six Scottish ships which were supposedly trading with France in violation of the treaty. Henry let it be known

---

[5]*Hamilton Papers*, 1:664-5, Sadler to Henry 8, 29 August 1543; *Sadler's State Papers*, 1:277-82, Sadler to Henry 8, 28 August 1543; Additional 32,651 folios 243-44, Arran to Henry 8, 17 August 1543 and folios 298-99, Arran to Henry 8, 31 August 1543.

[6]*Hamilton Papers*, 2:2, Sadler to Henry 8, 1 September 1543.

[7]Ibid., p. 4.

that the crews of the ships spoke harshly of Arran and his party--calling them "arrant and rank traitours to the quene and the realm"--undoubtedly to make the governor acquiesce more readily in this high-handed action. Henry's plan, however, backfired. The treaty had not been ratified by either the Scots or the English when the seizure of the merchant vessels occurred. The Scots, therefore, had reason to be upset, for it was becoming clear that Henry was not going to abide by rules, treaty or otherwise, in regard to their kingdom.[8]

As the cardinal's followers increased into a truly threatening nationalist party opposed to English encroachment and as the prospects for a revival of his original regency council increased, Arran felt himself intensely isolated in spite of assurances from the king's party. The governor had acted in good faith with Henry in regard to the completion of the treaties of peace and marriage. His desire for a prorogation to ratify them in hopes of securing the presence of Beaton's party in full parliament and to lay satisfactory hostages for keeping the terms of the agreement were indicative of this. The fact that he was also playing for time was irrelevant.[9] For Arran's temporizing policy did not necessarily imply total abandonment of the king, although it actually served the interests of the cardinal and the pro-French party.

Now, however, Henry was too demanding in dealing with the Scots. He was clearly disturbed when Arran agreed to the formation of a new advisory council as well as to new custodians for the young queen. Nevertheless,

---

[8]Royal Ms. 18 B VI folio 156, Arran to Henry 8, 16 August [1543]; *Hamilton Papers*, 1:638, Henry 8 to Sadler, 16 August 1543; *Letters and Papers*, vol. 18, pt. 2: xvii-xix for a more elaborate discussion of this important seizure; also Knox, *History*, 1:47 and 50, which is quite inaccurate concerning this matter.

[9]Henderson, *Mary Queen of Scots*, 1:34-35; *Hamilton Papers*, 1:lix.

warnings to proceed with caution in rectifying these unpleasantries went unheeded by the king. On 31 August, the English privy council wrote to Sadler instructing him what to advise Arran, who was believed to be in the north of Scotland. The governor should take control of Stirling and remove young Mary to a place more hospitable to English interests. Also, her attendants representing the cardinal's faction should be replaced by individuals more amenable to Henry.[10]

This advice to disregard his agreement with Beaton's party helped convince Arran of Henry's true intentions. Treaty or not, the English king was determined to get his own hands on his young grandniece as soon as possible.[11]

On 3 September, one day after acknowledging Arran's ratification, Henry's designs upon the Scottish realm took their toll as the man who had nourished English expectations for the past eight months left the king's fold. The day of defection long anticipated by many of Henry's more perceptive adherents had finally arrived--instead of the governor capturing the cardinal, the cardinal had captured the governor.

Arran, accompanied by a few attendants, claimed that he was going to visit his pregnant wife at Blackness, a few miles north of Linlithgow. This departure triggered rumors of actual revolt.[12] This time they turned out to be true. Leaving Blackness on 4 September, the governor met the cardinal and the earl of Moray with open arms at Callendar House on the road to Stirling. The

---

[10]Ibid., pp. 665-66, the privy council to Sadler, 31 August 1543.

[11]Ibid., lx.

[12]Additional 32,652 folio 24, Henry 8 to Arran, 3 September 1543; *Hamilton Papers*, 2:14, Sadler to Suffolk and Tunstall, 4 September 1543.

"verie freendelie imbracynges" between these two major Scottish rivals signalled the beginning of a momentous twist in Anglo-Scottish relations.

The abbot of Paisley and the governor's secretary, David Paniter, both sympathetic to the cardinal and instrumental in Arran's defection, were sent back to Linlithgow for the purpose of stopping those noble supporters of the governor who were gathering forces for a military confrontation between the two parties. These lords were told to prepare themselves for a convention whereby the two groups would settle all matters and divisions between them.[13]

The complete details of Arran's change of allegiance are found in a letter from the ever-perceptive Parr to Suffolk. The substance of the correspondence was gathered from an informant named Sandy Pringill. In this about face, the governor agreed to the delivery of Scottish castles, strongholds, and fortresses to Beaton and the earls--Lennox, Huntly, Argyle, and Bothwell. Instead of fulfilling his promise to do this for Henry, Arran in an unprecedented display of inconstancy pledged them to the prelate. The governor also confessed to his new Catholic friends that the English king had urged him to suppress many abbeys and friaries. By Arran's own consent, the friary of Dundee had been sacked.

Soon after making his confession, the governor, accompanied by the aforementioned lords, travelled to the friary at Stirling where he received open penance and made an oath that he would never commit such atrocities again. Rather, Arran would lend his support to the Catholic faith, including its orders of monks and friars. Thereafter, he was absolved by Beaton and the bishops in attendance, heard mass, and received communion. Argyle and Bothwell ". . .

---

[13]Ibid., 2:18-19, Sadler to Henry 8, 5 September 1543; *Sadler's State Papers*, 1:282-4, Sadler to Henry 8, 5 September 1543.

helde the towell over his hede" as he took the sacrament. In the afternoon, the governor ". . . remytted and referred all his procedings and doinges to the ordre and advice" of the cardinal and his party--promising that he would not do anything without their advice and counsel.[14]

The cardinal, however, was no more sure of the governor's sincerity than others had been. In fact, Beaton suspicioned Arran's inconstancy so much that he managed to secure the governor's oldest son as a pledge of good faith. The young Hamilton was kept within Beaton's castle at St. Andrews.[15]

On Sunday, 9 September, at ten o'clock in the morning, young Mary was crowned queen of the Scots in the chapel at Stirling Castle. In a fitting display of royalty, Arran bore the crown, Lennox the scepter, and Argyle the sword. All noblemen not present at the queen's coronation were summoned to Edinburgh to appear before the new Scottish council.

Although Beaton and Arran were at times outwardly conciliatory towards Henry, differences were immediately perceived in the policies of the Scottish government now staffed with new recruits. Parr reported that the Scots had no intent to frame a peace with the English in any way other than they had done in the past. The Greenwich treaties were completely unacceptable to the Scottish government. Particularly offensive to it was the deliverance of young Mary as specified in the articles.[16]

---

[14]*Hamilton Papers*, 2:38, Parr to Suffolk, 13 September 1543.

[15]Ibid., p. 188, Sadler to Suffolk and Tunstall, 26 November 1543.

[16]Henderson, *Mary Queen of Scots*, 1:37-38; *Hamilton Papers*, 2:38-39, Parr to Suffolk, 13 September 1543.

This was a blow to Henry and his dwindling group of supporters within Scotland. The Douglases, including Arran's own wife, were disturbed by the governor's defection. An emotionally charged comment that this weeping woman made to her husband was in keeping with the opinions of others concerning him--"What goo ye aboute to doo that whiche ye have promysed? Though your cote be sure and strong, your herte is dulle and feynt. . . ."[17] Broken promises were plentiful. A list of those made by Arran to Henry was compiled in December, followed closely by rumors that a divorce between the governor and his wife was imminent.[18]

As the Scottish government reorganized itself, it found time to level its own complaints against Henry's kingdom to the English ambassador. Not only had Scottish merchant vessels been illegally seized, there had been the usual border skirmishes as well. Also, as if the Scots really cared, the English king, after all the trouble Scotland had gone to, had failed to ratify the treaties of marriage and peace. Sadler replied to this grievance by stating that since hostages had not been laid, which according to Henry was "the principall knott of the treaties," his monarch had deferred their ratification.[19]

Henry steadfastly maintained that it was due to the "negligence frailtie and mutabilitie" of Arran that his treaties had foundered. Perhaps this vacillating figure could be coerced back into the English fold. But even the king's own friends had deceived him. They had convinced Henry to trust the

---

[17]Ibid., p. 40, Parr to Suffolk, 13 September 1543.

[18]Ibid., pp. 247-8, notes from Arran's letters, December 1543 and p. 294, Hertford and others to Henry 8, 8 March 1544.

[19]Ibid., pp. 68-70, Sadler to Henry 8, 24 September 1543; *Sadler's State Papers*, 1:300-5, Sadler to Henry 8, 24 September 1543.

governor and to believe that his treaties would be easily accepted. Thus, the king's ultimate desire to subjugate Scottish independence would not be achieved as easily as he had hoped. Henry had been deceived, not the Scots. To rectify what they could of the situation, Henry's party would have to get both Beaton and Arran into its possession, or at least, to deprive them of all authority.[20]

The English monarch still nourished senseless dreams. To believe that his friends could depose a governor named by the three estates of parliament and to capture the strongest leader of the faction dedicated to the preservation of Scottish independence was absurd, even in such an unruly kingdom as this.

Although Henry had been prepared to achieve his purposes by force all along, calmer judgements had prevailed. The English king considered Arran's defection to be an obvious cause for a resumption of hostilities. Instead of relying upon diplomacy, Henry made it clear that he would resort to force in an effort to secure his designs. For the time being at least, the season of the year was argued as a reason against the king sending his army of invasion.[21] After all, the Scots had already been alienated enough by recent relations with the English. Their real punishment could wait until spring.

Arran's temporizing policy had served his nation well. He had continually delayed moving against Beaton until the peace and all its particulars were secure. But three days after the deadline of ratification, Arran allowed just the opposite of what he had consistently pledged to the credulous Sadler to occur. The cardinal had captured him, instead of his having captured the

---

[20]Additional 32,652 folios 131-34 secret minute for Arran, 24 September 1543; *Hamilton Papers*, 2:82-4, Henry 8 to Sadler, 30 September 1543.

[21]Ibid., pp. 100-101, Sadler to Henry 8, 13 October 1543.

cardinal. Could the governor ever be forgiven? His eventual confrontations with the forces of an intensely vengeful king were to suggest not. But despite this situation, the Scots did at least gain time to recoup their previous losses and to prepare themselves to meet the English in battle when it would again ensue.

Arran's defection should not be blamed for the wrath which Henry subsequently showered upon Scotland--for it was apparent that there was no other way in which Scottish independence could be preserved. Bloodshed would continue to be characteristic of Anglo-Scottish relations. Previous English monarchs had evidently realized the futility of this approach as had Henry-- hence his plan to proceed diplomatically rather than militarily. But when diplomacy failed, Henry was very willing to use this alternative measure regardless of its success in the past. Without Arran, Scotland would have probably paid its price in lives and destruction at a much earlier date, when the Scots were less able to defend themselves against English aggression. Whereas Henry's predecessors had failed, the incumbent English sovereign could perhaps have succeeded. During the early months of Arran's regency, immediately following the Scots' rout at Solway Moss, the death of their king, and the accession of an infant queen, the independence of the northern kingdom might have very easily been lost. Owing, however, in no small part to the governor, it was not.

Nevertheless, Henry had one consolation in Arran's defection. In view of their rival claims, it was unlikely that both the governor and Lennox could remain within the same camp. Therefore, soon after Arran's transfer of allegiance, Lennox moved into Henry's fold.[22] Unfortunately for the English, Lennox was a poor substitute for the governor. Arran held all the strongholds except Dumbarton, and was more inclined to heed advice than was Lennox.[23] Of course, Henry preferred puppets, in spite of his failure always to control their strings.

According to George Douglas, there were three things which the king could do to insure Lennox's loyalty. First, the earl should be allowed to marry Lady Margaret Douglas, Angus' daughter and Henry's own niece. Second, a convenient living should be given him in place of that which he could no longer expect from France. Third, Lennox should be helped in attaining his title as lawful governor and next in line to the Scottish succession.[24] Douglas hoped that Lennox could be as good an Englishman as he had been a Frenchman.

Despite the fact that Henry was comforted by Lennox's behavior, the king was disturbed to hear of the landing in Scotland during October of the French ambassadors, Monsieurs Jacques de la Brosse and Jacques Ménage, as well as the papal legate, Grimani.[25] Francis I had appointed these ambassadors

[22]Ibid., p. 61, Sadler to Henry 8, 20 September 1543, pp. 114-15, Henry 8 to Angus, Cassillis, and Glencairn, 19 October 1543, and pp. 131-32, Sadler to the privy council, 30 October 1543; *Sadler's State Papers*, 1:299, Sadler to Henry 8, 20 September 1543 and pp. 325-27, Sadler to the privy council, 30 October 1543.

[23]Gladys Dickinson, ed., *Two Missions of Jacques de la Brosse: An Account of the Affairs of Scotland in the Year 1543 and the Journal of the Siege of Leith, 1560*, Scottish Historical Society Publications, third series, vol. 36 (Edinburgh: University Press, 1942), p. 8. (Hereafter cited as *Missions of Jacques de la Brosse.*)

[24]*Hamilton Papers*, 2:101-3, Sadler to Henry 8, 13 October 1543; *Letters and Papers*, vol. 18, pt. 2:xxiv.

[25]Ibid., pt. 1:492, Grimani to Cardinal Farnese, 16 July 1543; *Hamilton Papers*, 1:656, the privy council to Sadler, 25 August 1543, 2:102-3, Sadler to Henry 8, 13 October 1543, and p.

to distribute both money and munitions, and to give annual pensions to Scottish nobles who would support France and work to frustrate English designs, particularly the treaties of peace and marriage. France was once again an active participant in the affairs of its partner in "the auld alliance."[26] The French mission, although successful in its ultimate goal of frustrating Henry's plans, suffered from an apparent failure to understand completely the intrigues of 1543. According to French reports, Lennox--"the cause of the dissension to Scotland and the rallying point for disaffection"--managed to get some of Francis' money and munitions only to use them against French interests.[27]

As the English position in Scotland deteriorated in the fall of 1543, the situation of Henry's ambassador became increasingly uncertain. Sadler, whose life had been threatened in the summer and who was the focal point of Scottish animosity in Edinburgh following the king's seizure of the merchant vessels, lived in continuous danger and fear.[28] Many of the inhabitants of the capital

---

108, Sadler to the privy council, 16 October 1543; Slavin, *Politics and Profit*, p. 126; also *Missions of Jacques de la Brosse* and Jules de La Brosse's *Histoire d'un Capitaine Bourbonnais au XVIe Siècle. Jacques de La Brosse, 1485 (?)--1562. Ses Missions en Écosse* (Paris: Librairie Ancienne Honoré Champion, 1929), are two excellent accounts of this important French mission to strife-torn sixteenth-century Scotland. (Hereafter cited as *La Brosse.*) *Sadler's State Papers*, 1:318-19, Sadler to the privy council, 16 October 1543.

[26]*Hamilton Papers*, 2:132, Sadler to the privy council, 30 October 1543; *Sadler's State Papers*, 1:325-28, Sadler to the privy council, 30 October 1543.

[27]*Missions of Jacques de la Brosse*, pp. 8-13 on Lennox and pp. 25, 31 and 33 of *Discours* in the work.

[28]*Hamilton Papers*, 2:106-7, Sadler to the privy council, 16 October 1543, pp. 120-1, Sadler to the privy council, 25 October 1543, and pp. 141-3, Sadler to the privy council, 6 November 1543; *Sadler's State Papers*, 1:317, Sadler to the privy council, 16 October 1543, pp. 320-2, Sadler to the privy council, 25 October 1543, pp. 328-9, Sadler to the privy council, 30 October 1543, p. 329, Sadler to the privy council, 6 November 1543.

city were so infuriated with the English that they wanted to hold Sadler hostage for the return of their ships.

An irate Henry wrote to the governor on 27 October reprimanding him for his recent actions and infidelity. Two weeks later Arran made a very stringent reply defending his conduct in the clearest of terms.[29]

According to the English ambassador in late October, the whole Scottish realm was inclined towards France as that nation required nothing of them but friendship. France had supplied Scotland with both necessary revenue and arms. The English, on the other hand, sought above all to subject the Scots to their rule by exerting superiority and domination over them. Hence, the Scots so detested and abhorred the English that Sadler believed that Henry's plan of subjugating Scottish independence by means of a marriage could never be achieved without resorting to force.[30]

Even Sadler's last refuge, Tantallon Castle, was not free from danger. On 11 December, George Douglas accompanied by a large retinue arrived to transport Sadler to safety in the border town of Berwick.[31]

On the same day as this evacuation, Arran and the Scottish parliament which had been in session at Edinburgh since 3 December, decided that the treaties with the English had expired. The parliament declared that Arran's

---

[29]Ibid., pp. 308-9, Sadler to the privy council, 27 September 1543; *Hamilton Papers*, 2:76, Sadler to the privy council, 27 September 1543; Additional 32,091 folio 136 and Sloane 3199 folio 236b, Henry 8 to Arran, 27 October 1543; Sloane 3199 folios 82 and 237b and Additional 32,653 folio 35, Arran to Henry 8, 10 November 1543.

[30]*Hamilton Papers*, 2:132, Sadler to the privy council, 30 October 1543; *Sadler's State Papers*, 1:325-7, Sadler to the privy council, 30 October 1543.

[31]Ibid., pp. 348-51, Sadler to Suffolk, 12 December 1543; *Hamilton Papers*, 2:221, Sadler to Suffolk, 12 December 1543.

government had acted in good faith with Henry in regard to the negotiation and ratification of the Greenwich treaties of peace and marriage. The English, however, had not reciprocated. Scottish merchants, along with their ships and goods, had been seized by the English and had not been restored. These Scots were being detained as enemies. Hence, Henry, not the Scots, had violated and broken the peace. Since the contract of marriage had been granted for the peace to be observed, it too had expired. In addition, the English king, unlike Arran, had not yet bothered to ratify the treaties.[32]

Parliament, upon the instigation of la Brosse and Menage, renewed its past treaties with France. Acting upon the request of the governor, Beaton was reinstated as chancellor and authority was given to prelates and ordinaries to prosecute heretics.[33]

As if this were not enough, Arran had written to Pope Paul III and the cardinal of Capri on 8 December expressing a need for money to meet the threat of Henry who sought to destroy Scotland's sovereignty and to overthrow its religion and obedience to Rome as well. Should the pope choose to grant the necessary revenue, the Scots would be bound to the papacy forever.[34]

In spite of these developments, Arran continued to press the English king

---

[32]Ibid., pp. 220-1, act of the Scottish parliament, 11 December 1543; also similarly in *Acts of the Parliaments*, 2:431.

[33]Ibid., pp. 431-2 and 442-3; *Letters and Papers*, vol. 18, pt. 2:268, on Scotland and France; Alexandre Teulet, ed., *Relations Politiques dé la France et de l'Éspagne avec l'Éscosse au XVIc Siècle, Papiers d'État, Pièces et Documents, Inédits ou Peu Connus Tirés des Bibliothèques et des Archives de France*, 5 vols. (Paris: Veuve Jules Renouard, 1862). 1:119-23; *La Brosse*, pp. 89-91.

[34]*Letters and Papers*, vol. 18, pt. 2:256, Arran to Paul 3 and Arran to the cardinal of Capri, 8 December 1543.

for an honorable diplomatic solution. Henry's heart, however, had hardened.[35]

What Henry had begun following his defeat of the Scots in the field at Solway Moss was now officially undone just over one year later. The English king had undoubtedly won the battle, but to his dismay, he had lost the war.

---

[35]Sloane 3199 folio 82, Arran to Henry 8, 21 December 1543.

CHAPTER VII

To Punish the Scots: War Begins Anew

Despite the unsettled conditions and skirmishes which prevailed following the major realignments of the summer and fall of 1543, there was still hope that the factious Scottish nobility could unite in support of the government. The Greenside agreement of 13 January 1544 suggested that such was still possible. A number of the king's friends not present at the December parliament, including Cassillis, Glencairn, and the representatives of Angus and Lennox met with commissioners of Arran's government and agreed to be loyal to their queen and to help the governor in defending the realm and its church against their "auld innemes"--the English. They were to be shown favor by Arran and his party. Charges of treason were also to be dropped against George Douglas, the governor's once most trusted counsellor.[1]

Henry was furious. But fortunately for the English king, the agreement was as sincere as an earlier plan of the cardinal was feasible. Beaton, so it seemed, hoped to reconcile the rival Scottish factions by an ingenious matrimonial scheme. Arran was to divorce his wife and marry the queen

---

[1]Sloane 3199 folio 82, Douglas to Suffolk, 15 January 1544; *State Papers*, 5:356, agreement between Arran and Angus, 13 January 1544.

dowager while Lennox was to be contracted in marriage to the young Mary. Lennox would be made lieutenant general of Scotland with real authority while Arran was to enjoy only the name of his office with a yearly stipend. Hence, all were to be friends, united in devotion to France and in hatred of England.[2]

Regardless of such protestations and schemes, Scotland enjoyed little respite from the sporadic military confrontations between the rival parties.[3] In March, Lennox, Angus, Cassillis, and Glencairn declared that they were in imminent danger. Arran and Beaton were preparing a great force against them. Despite their questionable conduct, they still sought Henry's help. The English king realized that only he could offer the aforementioned earls the military assistance that they so desperately needed. But first, their wavering loyalties, particularly Lennox's, must give way to absolute obedience to the English cause.[4] Although late March was hardly the season to send an expedition into Scotland, plans were already being formulated by the English to inflict their revenge upon the Scots.[5]

During the first week of April, Arran was busy besieging Glasgow, then held by Lennox.[6] Due to the help of two of Henry's so-called friends, Maxwell

---

[2]*Hamilton Papers*, 2:151, Sadler to Suffolk and Tunstall, 10 November 1543; *Sadler's State Papers*, 1:335-7, Sadler to Suffolk and Tunstall, 10 November 1543.

[3]Sloane 3199 folio 82, Douglas to Suffolk, 15 January 1544; *Hamilton Papers*, 2:250, Douglas to Suffolk, 15 January 1544.

[4]*State Papers*, 5:361-2, instructions to Wharton and Bowes, 26 March 1544.

[5]Ibid., and p. 360, Hertford and others to Henry 8, 8 March 1544; *Hamilton Papers*, 2:294, Hertford and others to Henry 8, 8 March 1544 and p. 304, Hertford and others to Henry 8, 20 March 1544.

[6]Ibid., p. 717, master of Morton to the council in the north, 5 April 1544.

and Angus, the governor was finally able to take the town and to besiege the castle. The slipperiness of the king's party is well-illustrated by a vivid description of the circumstances surrounding this event. Angus arrived in Hamilton where he stayed overnight with Arran and Maxwell. The next day he travelled home to Douglas where he gathered his supporters. They soon accompanied him back to Hamilton where the three earls along with their recruits prepared to take Glasgow on the following day. The town fell easily. Arran, Angus, and Maxwell and their followers also laid siege to the castle fortified by Lennox's party. That same night, following their successes at Glasgow, Henry's alleged friends--Angus and Maxwell--went into private consultation with the governor. Angus, in particular, was described as being in the greatest favor with the Scottish leader. Yet in spite of this, Arran brought the two earls back to Hamilton Castle where they were "put into ward." Although many men marvelled that the governor would do this to individuals who had helped him so much, it was supposed that this confinement could not have taken place without the earls' consent.[7] In addition, George Douglas was arrested, being released only after England's devastating invasion of Scotland in May, when Henry's so-called friends were once again loyal servants.[8]

The nature of Henry's Scottish friends was not conducive to the success of his scheme. He had followed his plan of peaceful deceit to subvert Scottish sovereignty with a group of unreliable assured lords for long enough and to no avail. When Henry did decide to act against the Scots, his wrath knew no

---

[7]*State Papers*, 5:367-69, the saying of Edward Storye, servant unto Lord Wharton, 6 April 1544.

[8]*Letters and Papers*, vol. 19, pt. 1:xvii-iii and xxiv-xxv.

limits. His northern neighbors who had so sharply rebuked both him and his plans in 1543 would be punished for God was on his side. The Scottish enemies--chief among them Arran and Beaton--must pay for their transgressions. The English were determined that the Scots should know that the main reasons for the destruction about to be unleashed upon their country were the governor and the cardinal. The English king could easily find excuses for his actions--the Scots must simply learn not to deal so lightly with him.[9]

Henry VIII's final campaigns against his northern neighbor were more devastating and brutal than any of the many other invasions of that kingdom. The English king wanted to pulverize Scotland--forcing her into either acquiescence or destruction.[10]

The military leader of these English invasions was Edward Seymour, earl of Hertford and future protector during the reign of Henry's son and successor, Edward VI. Born around 1500, he later studied at Oxford. In 1524, Seymour became a gentleman usher in Henry VIII's court. It was in 1525, however, as master of the horse to the duke of Richmond, the king's bastard, that he first attracted Henry's attention. Thereafter, he rose in favor with the monarch, being made a privy councillor in 1537.

On 10 April 1544, Hertford was sent explicit military instructions by the privy council. Because Henry intended personally to invade France in the summer, a main reason for sending his army into Scotland was ". . . to counfounde his ennemys there in such sorte and so to devaste their countrey" so that neither they nor their French and Danish allies might seriously invade or

---

[9]*Hamilton Papers*, 2:350, the privy council to Hertford, enclosure, 24 April 1544.

[10]Ferguson, *Relations*, p. 61.

harm England.[11] The king's backdoor must be secured.

Henry's orders knew no mercy. Hertford must ". . . put all to fyre and swoorde." In particular, the town of Edinburgh should be completely obliterated--creating an example of God's vengeance unleashed upon such a false and disloyal people. The castle there should be overthrown and destroyed, while Holyrood House was to be sacked. Outlying areas of the city were to be treated likewise. Leith was to be sacked and burned. All men, women, and children, without exception, were to be annihilated should they resist. Fife was to be similarly attacked and destroyed.

A major target was Beaton's town--St. Andrews. Nothing there should be spared, especially friends or relatives of the cardinal. Should the castle be taken, it was to be razed and destroyed piece by piece. In all of this, Hertford was to use his own discretion. Nothing was to be attempted which might not easily be accomplished.[12]

Hertford was also urged to be as cautious as possible of what strategic items he left behind for his enemies to take advantage of, as this was to be only a preliminary exercise for what Henry intended to do the following year. At that time he would have a better opportunity to invade.[13]

Hertford's first Scottish invasion met with great success. Although historians from the time of John Knox in the sixteenth century to Gordon Donaldson in the twentieth, have held that the Scots were taken by surprise when the English fleet of two hundred sail arrived in the Firth of Forth on

---

[11]*Hamilton Papers*, 2:325, privy council in Hertford, 10 April 1544.

[12]Ibid., p. 326.

[13]Ibid., pp. 325-6 and pp. 341-3, consultation of the council, 17 April 1544.

Saturday, 3 May, there is evidence to the contrary.[14]   For example, the accounts of the lord high treasurer of Scotland contain warnings of the approaching English dated 21 April and a few days later.[15]   Little good, however, did these messages do.

The English invasion force was quite impressive.   Three thousand horsemen in jacks with spears rode first, followed by eight score of the nobility and gentlemen dressed in coats of black velvet and chains of gold.   There were three trumpets and clarions as well as three officers of arms in their coats of arms, as well as a gentleman who carried a drawn sword.   Next, came the earl of Hertford, adorned in sumptuous attire with three pages of honor lavishly clothed and eight score of his servants in his livery.   Finally, there followed five thousand men of foot.[16]

On 4 May this army landed near Newhaven.   While marching towards Leith, it found a Scottish army of "6000 horsemen, beside footmen" which shortly fled, led by the reluctant pair, Arran and Beaton.   On 6 May, Edinburgh was won by assault.   Part of the city was burned, including Holyrood and the King's Palace adjoining it.   On 9 and 10 May the rest of the capital was burned,

---

[14]Knox, *History*, p. 56; Gordon Donaldson, *Scotland: James V to James VII*, the Edinburgh History of Scotland series, vol. 3 (Edinburgh and London: Oliver and Boyd, 1965), pp. 69-79. (Hereafter cited as Donaldson, *Scotland.*)

[15]Great Britain, Public Record Office, *Compota Thesaurariorum Regum Scotorum. Accounts of the Lord High Treasurer of Scotland*, eds. Thomas Dickson and James Balfour Paul, 11 vols. (Edinburgh: Her Majesty's Stationery Office, 1877-1916), 8:284 and 286. (Hereafter cited as *Accounts of the Treasurer.*)

[16]Beer, *Northumberland*, pp. 28-30; *Letters and Papers*, vol. 19, pt. 1:333-4, Hertford's invasion of Scotland, May 1544; also see The Maitland Club's *Selections from Unpublished Manuscripts in the College of Arms and the British Museum Illustrating the Reign of Mary Queen of Scotland*, ed. Joseph Stevenson (Glasgow: The Maitland Club, 1837), pp. 3-5. (Hereafter cited as Stevenson, *Selections.*)

as well as other areas. Meanwhile, Hertford's force was joined by four thousand light horsemen sent by Henry. According to one account:

> . . . the clere forsoke theyre shippes and sente them home laden with spoyle and gunshotte, and returnid hom on fote throwghe the mayne cuntrey of Scotland, burnynge bothe pyle, fortresse and towne which was in theyre waye, and lost skante xl persons.[17]

Ravaging continued as many other towns and villages along with a number of religious establishments were burned. English destruction knew no limits.[18] The young Scottish queen--Henry's most cherished prize--nonetheless, always eluded him. Reluctant, Arran and Beaton might very well be, but negligent of their young monarch, they were not. She was taken by the governor and the cardinal to Dunkeld for her greater protection.[19]

On 25 May Hertford wrote to his king acknowledging the thanks which Henry had expressed to him for such a thorough destruction of his neighbor from Leith to the borders.[20] Hertford's success had in fact convinced many Scots that neither Arran nor Beaton was the leader that their kingdom so desperately needed in facing its southern foe. Attention, therefore, began to turn towards one closest to the young Scottish sovereign--Mary of Guise, the queen

---

[17]Ibid., p. 5; *Letters and Papers*, vol. 19, pt. 1:334, Hertford's invasion of Scotland, May 1544.

[18]Ibid., plus pp. 330-33, the late expedition in Scotland to Lord Russell, May 1544; *Tudor Tracts, 1532-1588*, introd. A. F. Pollard (New York: E. P. Dutton and Co., n.d.), pp. 37-47. (Hereafter cited as *Tudor Tracts*.)

[19]*Hamilton Papers*, 2:372, Hertford to Henry 8, 15 May 1544.

[20]Ibid., p. 387, Hertford and others to Henry 8, 25 May 1544.

dowager.

A movement developed in late May to supplant Arran in office. On 3 June Douglas was present at the convention of nobles held in Stirling which suspended the governor from his office. He told the assembly that Arran:

> . . . vitht counsell off the Cardenell, hadde distrwyit this holle rowyme, that brake the pesse and contrake off mariage qwhilk vas takein vitht the Kinges mageste off Ingland; be resson off his falset the erme off Ingland vas commit and distrwyit ane gret parte off this contra, and farder sed on to hym that he vas parjurit and not ebille to bere the office.[21]

When confronted with this charge, Arran along with two companions left Stirling for Blackness Castle. The Scottish lords proceeded to discharge him from the government and to make announcements of the change in the principal towns. Arran was also summoned to appear before a parliament on 28 July to be formally removed from his office. This action was necessary because he had been chosen governor by the three estates of the realm. A number of the lords, as already noted, wanted to make Mary of Guise sole ruler. Douglas, however, being the good Englishman that he was, maintained that since she was a woman, she was too weak to govern. Hence, Angus, Huntly, Argyle, and Bothwell were recommended as regents to assist her. Douglas argued that Lennox should have priority over Bothwell--undoubtedly in an attempt to please Henry. The other lords would have agreed with this suggestion had not Lennox become such an important partner to English interests. Finally, an agreement was reached that joined the queen dowager with a council of sixteen--twelve earls and four

---

[21]Ibid., pp. 409-10, enclosure, George Douglas to Hertford, 11 June 1544.

bishops.[22]

The July parliament which was intended to depose the governor, however, failed to meet. In fact, the only official evidence of this movement against Arran is found in a letter from the child queen to Henry, asking for a safe-conduct and a one month truce for certain Scots to negotiate a peace. In the correspondence, the young queen notified her great uncle that Arran had been suspended from the office of governor. Replacing him was Mary's "derest mother and certen of the gretest nobles" of the realm.[23]

On 22 June, Angus reported that both Arran and the cardinal were trying to make whatever friends they could by "mony and solistacion in the starkest sort" to resist this movement against them.[24] However strong this rivalry was, Arran remained in a position which enabled him to make a plea to Paul III on 17 June concerning his brother's nomination to the bishopric of Dunkeld.[25] All was not lost.

Arran's conduct during the summer of 1544 was influenced by this rivalry as he remained in Edinburgh Castle away from all but his friends for a large portion of the time.[26] Yet, according to the author of the *Diurnal*, on the

---

[22]Ibid., p. 410 only; there is also another account of this assembly in *State Papers*, 5:391-4, the copy of the agreement made in the convention at Stirling, 10 June 1544.

[23]An undated manuscript in the Cotton collection, Caligula B IV, folio 262, describes the governor's retreat from the court; *Hamilton Papers*, 2:415, the Queen of Scots to Henry 8, 21 June 1544.

[24]Ibid., p. 416, Angus to Wharton, 22 June 1544.

[25]*Letters and Papers*, vol. 19, pt. 1:445, Arran to Paul 3, 17 June 1544.

[26]*Hamilton Papers*, 2:421, Shrewsbury and others to the council, 8 July 1544 and p. 437, Sir Ralph Evers to Shrewsbury, 1 August 1544.

last of July, the timid and vacillating governor acted boldly in Edinburgh as he made a heroic stand and prevented the queen dowager from meeting in parliament with the Scottish estates who would have tried to remove him from office.[27] In this instance, Arran's inclination towards inconstancy and weakness was probably rectified in no small measure by the strength, resolve, and encouragement of Beaton.[28] Soon thereafter, another parliament summoned to meet at Stirling to depose him failed to materialize.[29]

The queen dowager's following was entirely too diverse to form a true party. Concerning the major issues of church and foreign policy, no agreement within Mary's group could be found. Neither had an actual breach between the dowager and Beaton taken place. As far as foreign interests or intervention were concerned, the major personalities were not included among Mary of Guise's partisans. Beaton and Arran were both champions of the French alliance and interest, while Lennox and Glencairn were the only important friends that Henry could still trust in all of Scotland, the Douglases' unreliability already having been shown.[30]

---

[27]*Diurnal*, p. 34; *Accounts of the Treasurer*, 8:308.

[28]*Scottish Correspondence*, p. 64.

[29]*Hamilton Papers*, 2:449, Vicar of Evan to ?, 8 August 1544.

[30]Donaldson, *Scotland*, p. 70; *Foedera*, 15:22-6; *Letters and Papers*, vol. 19, pt. 1:324-5, Lennox and Glencairn, 17 May 1544 and xxvi; Edmund Lodge, editor, *Illustrations of British History, Biography, and Manners, in the Reigns of Henry VIII, Edward VI, Mary, Elizabeth, and James I, Exhibited in a Series of Original Papers, Selected from the Manuscripts of the Noble Families of Howard, Talbot, and Cecil; Containing, Among a Variety of Interesting Pieces, A Great Part of the Correspondence of Elizabeth, and Her Ministers, With George, the Sixth Earl of Shrewsbury, During the Fifteen Years in Which Mary Queen of Scots Remained in His Custody; With Numerous Notes and Observations*, 3 vols. (London: G. Nicol, 1791), 1:128. (Hereafter cited as Lodge, *Illustrations*.) *Hamilton Papers*, 2:452, Shrewsbury to the queen, 2

The confrontation between these two major factions occurred in November 1544. Arran summoned a parliament to meet in ravaged Edinburgh, the base of his power, on the sixth of the month. The queen dowager summoned her parliament to meet six days later at Stirling.[31] According to George Douglas, the governor held a greater advantage in that his parliament was scheduled to meet first:

> . . . ye suffyr the governor and thaym to convene befoyr yow the mast part of Skotland will cum to hym and than hawe ye lost yowr purpos to the grate deshonowr of yow and all yowr part takars and the destrwksion of this hayll rewlm.[32]

There was a great deal of truth in what Douglas advised Mary of Guise. On 7 November Arran's parliament issued summonses of treason against Douglas, Angus, and Bothwell. All acts of the pretended parliament in Stirling were to be annulled including above all those which attempted to suspend or discharge the governor from his office.[33] In an obvious move towards reconciliation, however, Arran commissioned a group of his followers to meet with the queen dowager in hopes that justice might be administered and a stronger front be displayed to the English thieves and traitors.[34]

September 1544; *State Papers*, 5:394; *Scottish Correspondence*, pp. 60-5.

[31]Lodge, *Illustrations*, 1:178; Stevenson, *Selections*, pp. 9-10; *Acts of the Parliaments*, 2:445-47; *Letters and Papers*, vol. 19, pt. 2:339 and 342.

[32]*Scottish Correspondence*, p. 109, Douglas to the queen dowager, 13 October 1544.

[33]*Acts of the Parliaments*, 2:445-47; *Letters and Papers*, vol. 19, pt. 2:342.

[34]Ibid., p. 344; *Acts of Parliaments*, 2:448.

Because of Beaton's intervention, a compromise between the two factions was finally arranged. The queen dowager was to be the principal figure of the sixteen lords of the council--without whose advice Arran could not act.[35] Beaton was amenable to the idea of co-operating with the headstrong dowager, although he would not allow himself to be subservient to her.[36] Hence, on 12 December, pardons for treason were granted to Douglas, Angus, and Bothwell, and remissions to Glencairn and Cassillis.[37] To close the confrontation, on 6 March 1545, Mary of Guise while at Stirling signed the following:

> Be it kend [etc.] ws Marie be the graice of God quein dowarire of Scotland, to be bondin and oblist and be the fayth in our body and be thir presentes bindis and oblises ws to oure richt weil beluuit cousin James erle of Arran gouernour of oure derres dochteris realme of Scotland, that we sall lelele and treuly keip and leile trew and affald part onto him in all his actionis.[38]

Due to the support that he received from his erstwhile opponent, Cardinal Beaton, Arran had weathered a major storm. Arran's government triumphed due to its control of both political and church patronage, its greater power to endure, its more united command, and its more advantageous strategical location--Edinburgh. Moreover, if Arran alone was not Mary of Guise's equal, Beaton was a match for her ally, Douglas, in both diplomacy and in unselfish

---

[35]*Hamilton Papers*, 2:491, Anonymous to the laird of Lessford, 23 November 1544.

[36]*Scottish Correspondence*, p. 65.

[37]*Acts of the Parliaments*, 2:450-1; *Letters and Papers*, vol. 19, pt. 2:442-3.

[38]*Historical Manuscripts Commission, Eleventh Report*, p. 36, bond by the queen dowager, 6 March 1545.

patriotism.[39]

Divisions within the northern kingdom had been healed. Now a more united Scotland could turn its attention against the ever-present threat of Henry's England. For the remaining months of his life, Beaton would hold such an upper hand in Scottish policies that he bears the distinction of having been successful in the onerous tasks of making it possible for Arran and Mary of Guise to work together and of gaining the support of the less-devoted adherents of the English cause.[40]

For the remainder of 1544, following Hertford's invasion, a desultory warfare of border-type raids took place between the Scots and the English.[41] The success of Hertford, for example, at Jedburgh let the English into planning similar attacks upon Kelso and Melrose. According to Sir Ralph Evers, the English warden of the middle marches, if those areas were destroyed as Jedburgh was, the Scots would "... have no meet place to lie any garrisons near the Borders."[42]

The unreliability of Henry's paroled prisoners and the Douglas brothers in particular continued to pose problems for the king. Angus was now serving his own nation in the capacity of lieutenant of the borders. Although Angus' brother, Sir George, continued to profess his loyalty to the English king, his conduct was by no means always indicative of this fact. Douglas, nevertheless,

---

[39] *Scottish Correspondence*, p.64.

[40] Donaldson, *Scotland*, p. 71.

[41] *Hamilton Papers*, 2:xxvi.

[42] *Letters and Papers*, vol. 19, pt. 2:101, the council with the queen to the council with the king, 5 September 1544.

was quite successful in explaining his conduct to Henry. He also succeeded in making amends for Angus' actions as well. Douglas had urged his brother to resign his commission, yet no appropriate man was found willing to accept it. Did patriotism suddenly mean something to the earl? For after this resignation was proposed, Arran and the council asked Douglas how Scotland was to be defended. Sir George sarcastically replied that it was the governor's duty to do so as ". . . he hade bothe the proffit and the plesour, and vas ane luste zung man, meit to be exersit in varefare."[43] Arran, nonetheless, refused to discharge Angus from office. Thus being the case, Douglas would persuade him to perform in a manner that would not cause Henry to complain--provided he was gracious to them and their friends.[44]

Douglas continued to offer his advice to the English king. One recommendation contained an illustration of what is meant by an assured Scot of non-noble rank. Henry should make proclamations on the borders in which he declared to those who supported the Greenwich treaties that they would be shown favoritism and would be given protection by the English. Those who refused, however, would be persecuted with "faire and sworde to the moste extremite."[45] Should the king follow this suggestion of Douglas, his designs would be more easily accomplished for Henry's cruelty showered both upon his friends and his enemies had been so great that all of Scotland now believed that if the English became their masters every man, woman, and child would surely die. Finally Douglas cautioned, "Veisdome, mixte vith forse, ville helpe miche

---

[43]*State Papers*, 5:413, Douglas to Sir Ralph Evers, February 1545.

[44]Ibid.

[45]Ibid., plus p. 414.

in gret affaires. . . ."[46]

Such evidence together with his efforts to seek the Arran government's favor clearly prove that George Douglas was as crafty as Henry himself. Even more interesting is the fact that Henry seemingly believed Douglas's professions. On 19 February 1545, the English king wrote him, pardoning his past and restoring him to favor. Henry still had hope for his peace and marriage treaties with the Scots.[47]

Arran's government wanted to discuss peace as well, but not at Henry's price of having the Scottish prisoners returned to England first. Douglas "loyally" reported this desire to the English king while he was at Lauder, on the borders, where he had accompanied Arran to repel an attack.[48]

Eight days after Douglas's pardon, Arran's forces scored their greatest military triumph against the forces of Henry VIII. Unfortunately, the details of the Scots' rout of the English at Ancrum Moor, near Jedburgh, on 27 February 1545 are uncertain because of conflicting sixteenth-century accounts.[49]

What probably occurred is that the English succeeded in devastating Melrose, where the tombs of the Douglas family were desecrated. Upon their return from this expedition, the English encountered the Scots under the leadership of Arran and Angus. Both Sir Ralph Evers and Sir Brian Layton, the

---

[46]Ibid. These citations of Douglas to Evers were sent enclosed with correspondence of Douglas to Henry 8 dated 15 February. See also *Letters and Papers*, vol. 20, pt. 1:88-9.

[47]*State Papers*, 5:415-7, Henry 8 to Douglas, 19 February 1545.

[48]Ibid., pp. 417-8, Douglas to Henry 8, 25 February 1545; *Letters and Papers*, vol. 20, pt. 1:113 and xviii-xx and xxiii.

[49]See *Letters and Papers*, vol 20, pt. 1:xxiii-xxvii for a good account of the controversy surrounding the battle.

captain of Norham Castle, were killed, along with others of lesser rank. The Scots also took a sizeable number of English prisoners who could be used as possible exchanges for the pledges of those prisoners taken at Solway Moss.[50]

An interesting sidelight concerning both the governor and Angus is provided in one of the few known details surrounding this outstanding Scottish triumph. Following the battle, Arran took an acquaintance of the warden to that part of the field where the slain lay. The governor showed him Evers' body, whereupon the man confirmed his identity. As tears ran down his cheeks, Arran remarked:

> 'God have mercy on him, for he was a fell cruell man, and over cruell, which many a man and fatherles barne might new. And welaway! that ever such slaughter and blood sheding shulde be amongst Christen men.'[51]

After this, Arran turned his back and was later met by Angus who asked him, ". . . if he were merye?" The governor replied, "'My lorde, I am moche the meryer for you. . . .'" Thereupon, he took Angus:

> . . . about the necke, and kyssed him xx tyems, sayeng,--Wo wourth him that caused him to have any suspicion or mistrust in the said erle for Englondes cause, for he had that day shewed a

---

[50]Ibid., xxv; *Hamilton Papers*, 2:562-63, Cuthbert Layton and William Redman to Tunstall, 1 March 1545, pp. 561-62, Shrewsbury and others to Henry 8, 1 March 1545, p. 563, Shrewsbury and others to Henry 8 again, 1 March 1545, and pp. 581-82 Gilbert Swynhoo to Shrewsbury, 13 March 1545.

[51]Ibid., p. 565, Shrewsbury and others to Henry 8, 3 March 1545.

trew partie and don a grete good dayes worke to Scotlande.[52]

In response, Angus replied, ". . . that God knew and shulde judge his parte and loyaltee to his natif countrey."[53] In truth, the success of the Scots can be attributed not so much to Arran and Angus, who was undoubtedly seeking revenge upon the English for their destruction of the Douglas tombs, as to a number of Scots from Teviotdale who were assured to Henry only out of fear.[54]

    This Scottish success enraged Henry. Although the king was still confident that the northern kingdom could be crushed, he did not know how much more power it had to inflict additional annoyance upon England.[55] Arran's ability, however, to follow up this victory was hindered by religious dissension, distrust, and traditional private feuds within Scotland.[56]

    Angus' unreliability, in particular, restrained the governor's action. Although the Douglas brothers' support apparently continued to oscillate between the two factions, Henry persisted in his attempts to accomplish a large part of his designs by using the assured Scots in securing his treaties of marriage and peace. Such dreams proved illusory. On 20 April, Cassillis, then one of the king's more reliable Scots, wrote to Henry in cypher signifying that the governor, the queen dowager, and the cardinal remained as opposed to him as

---

[52]Ibid.

[53]Ibid.

[54]Ibid., and p. 567, Shrewsbury and other to Henry 8, 5 March 1545.

[55]*Letters and Papers*, vol. 20, pt. 1:xxvi.

[56]*Scottish Correspondence*, p. 122.

ever.[57]

Why should Arran be interested in the English marriage? The governor had his own bond which forced a number of Scots to support his eldest son's marriage to the queen. His dream of 1543, before Henry upset it with the English scheme, once again seemed capable of realization. Owing to great offers and fair words, Arran was so successful in this endeavor that by October 1545, it could be said that the greater part of both the temporal and spiritual estates had consented to his bond.[58] By doing this, Arran was attempting to build a strong moderate party which would be associated with his own political interests. The center of his activities was in the west country, especially in Hamilton and Paisley, where his family's influence remained the strongest.[59] The Scottish governor still had not abandoned the idea that he could in some way be his own man.

Despite such activity, there were still those few friends of Henry who continued to favor the Greenwich treaties. They thought that the English king might better achieve his plans by an invasion of Scotland by sea.[60]

Reports of impending French support coupled to their own victory at Ancrum Moor stiffened the resistance of Arran's government to Henry's

---

[57]*State Papers*, 5:424-6, Cassillis to Henry 8 in cypher, 2 April 1545, pp. 431-2, the privy council to Cassillis, 10 April 1545 and pp. 437-9, Cassillis to Henry 8 in cypher, 20 April 1545.

[58]*Scottish Correspondence*, p. 147, John Somerville to the queen dowager, 21 October 1545; *Historical Manuscripts Commission, Eleventh Report*, p. 36; Donaldson, *Scotland*, p. 71.

[59]*Scottish Correspondence*, p. 124.

[60]*State Papers*, 5:437-9, Cassillis to Henry 8 in cypher, 20 April 1545.

renewed desires.[61] In addition, the arrival of French military and financial assistance under the auspices of Lorges de Montgomery, persuaded Hertford that a planned second invasion should begin at an earlier date.[62]

According to English intelligence, Lorges landed at Dumbarton with three thousand men, of which five hundred were horsemen. He also came with five thousand crowns for Arran along with a hundred men to wait upon the governor at the French king's expense. Four thousand crowns were to be distributed to Angus and George Douglas with thanks for their recent service rendered against England. Angus received the "Ordre of the Coclee" along with a collar of gold and a message ". . . that he shall never lakk suche honour and pleasure as the Frenche King can do for hym."[63] The Douglases had the best of both worlds as a result of their oscillating conduct.[64]

The Scots appreciated Francis I's generosity. On 26 June the Scottish privy council, including George Douglas, met at Stirling and declared that as a result of such friendship, Scotland was willing to do its utmost either to defend itself, or to invade England. A few days later, the privy council named Angus and others to meet with Arran, the queen dowager, and the cardinal to discuss

---

[61]*Letters and Papers*, vol. 20, pt. 1:442, the privy council of Scotland, 7 June 1545.

[62]*State Papers*, 5:457-8, Hertford to Paget, 10 June 1545 and pp. 458-9, intelligences of Lord Wharton to Hertford, 10 June 1545.

[63]Ibid., and pp. 459-60, the credence of Arche Were to Wharton, 12 June 1545.

[64]See Donaldson, *Scotland*, pp. 72-3, on bribery during Mary Queen of Scots' minority. For example, Donaldson maintains that a major factor in the failure of Henry's plans to subvert Scottish independence lay in the fact that he was defeated at his own game of bribing the Scots.

the conduct of their war.[65]

Before the end of June, the council also decided that by 28 July, an army of the whole realm should be raised from all men between the ages of sixteen and sixty.[66] On 29 June those plans received official approval.[67]

Anglo-Scottish relations were significantly influenced by Scotland's diplomatic relationship with England's ally, the Holy Roman Emperor Charles V. In May 1544, Charles had yielded to English pressure, declaring the Scots his enemies. This declaration of war led to a break in the traditional commercial relations between Arran's kingdom and Flanders. The Scots, nonetheless, understood that the action had been taken reluctantly and only as a political necessity. In return for this declaration, Charles tried to get Henry to make a similar one against the emperor's old enemy, Christian III of Denmark--a traditional ally of the Scots. The emperor recognized Christian only as the duke of Holstein for the Hapsburgs claimed sovereignty over the Danes.

On 23 May 1544, however, matters were partially settled when Charles signed the treaty of Spires with the Danes, granting a perpetual peace and free traffic between the two realms.[68] Arran's kingdom was not overlooked as the

---

[65] *Acts of the Parliaments*, 2:594-97; *Letters and Papers*, vol. 20, pt. 1:504; Great Britain, Public Record Office, *The Register of the Privy Council of Scotland*, ed. John Hill Burton and Donald Masson, 14 vols. (Edinburgh: Her Majesty's General Register House, 1877-1898), 1:6, 26 June 1545. (Hereafter cited as *Register*.)

[66] Ibid., p. 8, 28 June 1545; *Acts of the Parliaments*, 2:595-96; *Letters and Papers*, vol. 20, pt. 1:508.

[67] Ibid., p. 509; *Acts of the Parliaments*, 2:596; *Register*, 1:8, 29 June 1545.

[68] *Letters and Papers*, vol. 19, pt. 1:xxix-xxx and p. 305, the emperor's declaration against the Scots, 7 May 1544, p. 349, concerning Charles 5 and Denmark, 23 May 1544 and vol. 20, pt. 1:xxxv.

treaty recorded that the Scots had committed hostilities against the Low Countries, and were, hence, the emperor's enemies. Denmark could not show any favor to Scotland, although navigation between the two kingdoms was not to be interdicted.[69]

Charles also cultivated better relations with France. In fact, the English king had proven to be a rather disappointing ally of the empire. Instead of assisting Charles in an attack upon Paris during the course of the war against the Valois, Henry had turned his attention towards enlarging his French territory, the Calais bridgehead. As a result of this independent course of aggression, the English gained Boulogne. Hence, the emperor made his peace with Francis in 1544, well before Henry did. Following the treaty of Crépy, Arran, on 1 January 1545, sent his secretary, David Paniter, in the role of ambassador to congratulate the emperor on this achievement and to beg him, since Charles' attitude towards Scotland was based on mere political necessity, to remain friendly with the northern kingdom. In the course of his travels, the Scottish ambassador also visited the king of France.[70]

As a result of these developments, the state of war between the empire and Scotland remained essentially nominal although appearances were maintained. The ancient alliances between the house of Burgundy and the kingdom of Scotland could not be renewed at that time, just as the Scots could not be comprehended in the Crépy peace.[71] Nevertheless, a definite

---

[69]Ibid., vol 19, pt. 1:349, Charles 5 and Denmark, 23 May 1544.

[70]*Spanish Calendar*, 8:1, Mary Queen of Scots to Charles 5, 1 January 1545, footnote as well; Elton, *Reform and Reformation*, pp. 307-11.

[71]*Letters and Papers*, vol. 20, pt. l:xxxvii and 290, "treaty" between Charles 5 and Scotland, 28 April 1545.

rapprochement between Scotland and the Holy Roman Empire disturbed Henry who had learned that there was "great practice with" Charles among the Scots, possibly including negotiations for a marriage between the young queen of Scots and one of the sons of the emperor's brother, Ferdinand.[72] Even more disquieting was the fact that news of this situation came in the wake of Ancrum Moor. The spring of 1545 was indeed unseasonably cold for the English monarch.[73]

So well were the affairs of Scotland progressing that Cardinal Beaton could write to Paul III on 6 July that the Scots were much better off than they were, as the quarrels among the nobles had been appeased and heresy was nearly extinguished.[74]

As the Scots, with assistance from France, continued preparations for their invasion of England in the summer of 1545, Hertford was once again making plans for his second major assault against them. The Englishman, however, had again altered his scheme. Instead of acting earlier, his expedition was deferred until September when he would be moving during harvest time and, hence, could cause more destruction.[75]

Despite Beaton's assurances to Paul III, the Scottish nobility remained disunited. Treason ran rampant in particular quarters. On 16 August, the Douglases and Cassillis wrote in cypher to Hertford in hopes of furthering

---

[72]Ibid., p. 338, the privy council to Wotton, 4 May 1545.

[73]Lacey Baldwin Smith, *Henry VIII: The Mask of Royalty* (Boston: Houghton Mifflin Company, 1971), p. 212.

[74]*Letters and Papers*, vol. 20, pt. 1:555, Cardinal Beaton to Paul 3, 6 July 1545.

[75]*State Papers*, 5:491-92, Hertford to Henry 8, 14 August 1545.

English plans. The invasion force should hastily proceed to both the east and west borders for harvest time. The force should be prepared to remain there for a lengthy period. Without such an extended stay, Henry's designs would suffer. Reiterating earlier suggestions, Hertford should declare to the Scots that it was not his intention to harm those who supported the Greenwich treaties of peace and marriage.[76]   Furthermore, these Scotsmen maintained that they had thwarted their kingdom's last feeble attempt of the summer to invade England.[77]

According to an English intelligence report on the continent, Henry now had greater cause to be optimistic than he had had in late winter and spring of the year. The French had been able to do little for the Scots who had recently invaded England for a mere six hours only to be driven back in shame. On the other hand, Henry had a strong following of both Scottish nobles and so-called savages of whom eight thousand were reported to have entered voluntarily into his service.[78]

Just as this report was good news to the English, so too were the results of Hertford's second invasion. In fact, he enjoyed such success in burning and destroying the countryside that there was agreement among those on the border, ". . . that there was not somoche hurte don in Scotland with fyere at one roode this hundred years, except the last journey to Edenburghe."[79]

Henry was well pleased with Hertford's revenge upon the Scots.

---

[76]Ibid, p. 498, Angus, Douglas, Cassillis, etc. to Hertford, 16 August 1545.

[77]Ibid.

[78]*Spanish Calendar*, 8:240, Scepperus to Schore, 21 August 1545.

[79]*State Papers*, 5:517-19, Hertford to Henry 8, 13 September 1545.

According to Hertford, his wanton destruction once again caused great disunity in the northern kingdom. Arran, unable to resist the English in battle, was described as being sick with melancholy. In view of the situation, both noblemen and commoners were so disobedient to him that Hertford concluded the Scots could not threaten England during the winter. Also the French found such misery and scarcity in the kingdom that they were weary, just as the Scots had grown weary of them. Even Lorges wanted to return to France. Finally, as if the English destruction and the disagreements between the Scots and their French allies were not enough, Hertford now reported that strife-torn Scotland faced the threat of the plague.[80]

Hertford had been joined in his invasion by Lennox in the west country. The latter was assisted by several Scottish clans in a raid on the island areas of Arran, Bute, and parts of Argyll. Donald, the earl of Ross, sometimes styled "the lord of the isles," along with his barons, had their names subscribed, with "hand at ye pen" as they could not write, to a bond pledging their support to the English king and Lennox. These highlanders, or savages, as continental sources called them, were to be used as Lennox, fully recognized as the second person of the Scottish realm, commanded.[81]

The lord of the isles having received one thousand crowns as a reward, along with the promise of a two thousand crown pension, was glad to assist Lennox, the true governor of Scotland. The lord and four thousand of his men would be Henry's subjects under Lennox's command, supporting the king's plan

---

[80]Ibid, 5:539-43, Hertford to Paget, 5 October 1545.

[81]Ibid., 5:477-78, Henry 8 and the lord of the isles, in the earl of Rosse, etc., to McAlister and McLean, 28 July 1545; Donaldson, *Scotland*, p. 72.

concerning Mary's marriage, as in all other matters.[82] Unfortunately for the English, when the lord of the isles died, so too did his insurrection. Scotland's fate would not be determined in its West Highlands.[83]

If Henry's efforts did not succeed in the Scottish Highlands during 1545-46, he did achieve a major triumph by helping to secure the death of his arch-enemy, Cardinal Beaton. Known plots had been laid against this prelate as early as April 1544. These plots had been approved by Henry, with the knowledge of such important officers of state as Sir Ralph Sadler.[84]

Protestantism in Scotland, contrary to what the cardinal had reported to the pope in the summer of 1545, was spreading. As late as 1 March 1546, one of the most important of Scottish religious reformers--George Wishart--still preached in the streets, although on that date, he was arrested and burned on charges of heresy. Perhaps Arran should have used Wishart as a bargaining point, rather than consenting to his death. Partly because of this act, Beaton was murdered in St. Andrews Castle some eight weeks later.

There is not much evidence to suggest that Beaton's assassination on 29 May 1546 was directly related to earlier plots against him. Fifty pound rewards, however, were given by the English to at least two of those involved, the master of Grange and the laird of Brunstone. Nevertheless, both the religious and

[82]*Letters and Papers*, vol. 20, pt. 2:18-19, lord of the isles, three documents, 5 August 1545; *State Papers*, 5:482-85.

[83]Donaldson, *Scotland*, p. 72; *Letters and Papers*, vol 21, pt. l:xlvi.

[84]*State Papers*, 5:377-78, Hertford to Henry 8, 17 April 1544 and pp. 449-51, the privy council to Hertford, 30 May 1545.

political implications of the cardinal's death were clear.[85] Personal motives may have also prompted some of the cardinal's assassins--anticipation, for example, that Beaton, aware of their plots, was preparing himself for actions against them.[86]

Regardless, the cardinal's assassination does not appear to have had a broad base of support nor to have commanded influential assistance within or without Scotland to usher in a revolution.[87] Even Knox, no great admirer of the cardinal, referred to the assassins as "men without god."[88]

Plans for the Scottish queen's marriage were affected by Beaton's death. His murderers agreed to support Henry's scheme of betrothing her to his son. In reaction, Arran's council at Stirling made Angus, Cassillis, Maxwell, and Douglas affirm the Scottish parliament's rejection of the Greenwich treaties on 11 June. These nobles also renounced all bonds that they had entered into with the English king. Arran, also at this meeting of the Scottish privy council, discharged the bond made with him by certain nobles concerning the queen's marriage to his son. Likewise, all bonds made to the queen dowager to the

---

[85]Donaldson, *Scotland*, p. 74; Also see Ridley, *Knox*, pp. 45-46 and Knox, *History*, 1:76-78; *Letters and Papers*, vol 21, pt. 1:lii-liii.

[86]Donaldson, *Scotland*, p. 75; Great Britain, Public Record Office, *Registrum secreti sigilli regum Scotorum: The Register of the Privy Seal of Scotland*, ed. James Beveridge, 7 vols. (Edinburgh: Her Majesty's Stationery Office, 1908-65), 4:no. 152, 7 March 1549, no. 715, 6 May 1550, and no. 1877, 11 February 1553.

[87]Donaldson, *Scotland*, p. 75; *State Papers*, 5:561, to Wharton, 30 May 1546.

[88]Knox, *History*, 1:97.

contrary were annulled.[89]

No chances were taken by Arran's government, for Scotland was in a state of deep political disarray. Beaton's death left a void which had to be filled. For the first time since his defection to the cardinal in September 1543, Arran was free of the prelate. Beaton's death, however, was no blessing to Arran. The coming months would be most difficult for the Scottish governor as he attempted to do what he could to make good the loss of this nationalistic leader.

The English king, on the other hand, was naturally pleased with the cardinal's elimination. A most important link in the chains which had shackled his Scottish designs was now severed. The rejoicing surrounding this event, however, proved to be short lived. Eight months later Henry himself would be dead--gone without ever having seen his cherished dream to subvert Scottish independence come to fruition. There was little mourning in the northern kingdom during that cold winter in which Henry VIII took his final breath.

---

[89]*Foedera*, 15:132-34; Donaldson, *Scotland*, p. 75; *Letters and Papers*, vol 21, pt. 1:520; *Register*, 1:29-30, 11 June 1546.

CHAPTER VIII

War Continues

The murder of Cardinal Beaton in the late spring of 1546 seemed a triumph for the English king. The cardinal's assassins held St. Andrews Castle for fourteen months. The fortress could serve as a major base of operations for the English on the east coast of Scotland, just as Dumbarton Castle, in the hands of Lennox, would serve for a much shorter time on the west coast. Moreover, an important hostage for this party had been found within St. Andrews. He was Arran's eldest son, who had been kept by the cardinal as a pledge of the governor's sincerity. This situation clearly limited Arran's ability to act quickly and decisively in regard to St. Andrews, unlike Dumbarton, which was recovered during the summer of 1546.[1]

Nevertheless, Arran's government attempted to solve this difficult problem. On 30 July, the Scottish parliament and lords of the privy council, Cassillis and both Douglases, met at Edinburgh and issued summonses of treason against those who participated in the slaughter of the cardinal and who held St. Andrews Castle. A proclamation was to be made against harming them

---

[1]*Letters and Papers.* vol. 21, pt. 2:2-3, Arran to the pope and the cardinals, 1 September 1546.

in hopes that they could be persuaded to surrender.[2] The new occupants of St. Andrews became known as the Castilians--holding the castle on into mid-summer 1547 with periodic assistance from English ships laden with items to succor them.[3]

As Arran himself maintained, Beaton's murder was not only a temporal crime but a spiritual one as well. Therefore, by the end of July, a sundry assortment of prelates and nobles of the Scottish realm had found sufficient cause to issue summonses of treason against Leslie, the actual slayer of the cardinal, and his accomplices.[4] As so often within clan-ridden Scotland, disaster had bred cohesion.

By 9 August the spirituality had consented to a remission provided the pope granted the assassins an absolution. Parliament, nonetheless, decreed that should these men fail to keep the promise to surrender Arran's son and the castle, this concession would be voided.[5]

The Scottish government in August also made necessary preparations for taxation and for the mustering and quartering of troops intended to besiege and recover the stronghold at St. Andrews. Desiring to detract from the importance of the Hamilton hostage, the Scottish parliament decreed that as long as he

---

[2]*Acts of the Parliaments*, 2:466-68; *Register*, 1:31-32, 30 July 1546; *Letters and Papers*, vol. 21, pt. 1:669, 30 July 1546.

[3]Ibid., pt. 2:49, council with the king to the council in London, 18 September 1546, pp. 49-50, on St. Andrews castle, September 1546, p. 52, Selve to Francis 1, 19 September 1546, and p. 214, Selve to Francis 1, 28 November 1546; Odet de Selve, *Correspondence politique 1546-49*, ed. G. Lefèvre-Pontalis (Paris: 1888), pp. 31-32, Selve to Francis 1, 19 September 1546 and pp. 66-67, Selve to Francis 1, 28 November 1546. (Hereafter cited as *Selve*.)

[4]*Letters and Papers*, vol 21, pt. 1:672, 31 July 1546; *Register*, 1:33, 31 July 1546.

[5]*Letters and Papers*, vol 21, pt. 1:719, 9 August 1546; *Acts of the Parliaments*, 2:469-70.

remained in captivity, he would be excluded from his father's rights, including his claim to the crown which should go to his next brother.[6]

By the end of October, the fortification had been so closely besieged that it could not be supplied by sea. The governor had placed mines near the foot of the castle's tower in hopes of capturing the fortification.[7]

Criticism, nonetheless, of Arran's military strength mounted because he was never able to take the stronghold during the year.[8] Although Arran was no military genius, there were reasons for his lack of success in regard to St. Andrews. Fear for the safety of his son influenced his lack of activity while rumors of yet a third major English invasion distracted his attention. On 19 December the Scottish privy council finally decided to come to terms with the besieged rather than risk the castle and the young Hamilton falling into Henry's possession. Time and money necessitated this action which went against the governor's wishes. Accounting for the effort put into the siege, the privy council's register simply recorded: that which ". . . is unable to be gottin bot be hungir quhilk will noct be haistelie done."[9]

A truce was finally arranged. After rounds of negotiating, it was agreed that the Protestant occupants could keep the castle and Arran's son until

---

[6]Ibid., pp. 471-74; *Letters and Papers*, vol. 21, pt. 1:728-29, 14 August 1546, p. 740, 21 August 1546 and pp. 747-48, 24 August 1546; *Register*, 1:38-39, 21 August 1546 and pp. 39-41, 24 August 1546.

[7]*Letters and Papers*, vol. 21, pt. 2:185, Selve to Francis 1, 10 November 1546; *Selve*, pp. 53-55, Selve to Francis 1, 10 November 1546.

[8]*Scottish Correspondence*, pp. 208-9, Methven to the queen dowager, 31 December 1547.

[9]*Letters and Papers*, vol. 21, pt. 2:295, 19 December 1546; *Register*, 1:57-58, 19 December 1546.

absolution from the pope arrived, provided they gave pledges for their own sincerity.[10]   In addition, neither they nor anyone associated with them would ever be pursued by the law for the cardinal's murder.   They would be able to enjoy both spiritual and temporal commodities which were possessed before their crime, just as though it had not been committed.   Finally, as the besieged had a strong need for food and drink, they were granted the right to replenish the castle.

As John Knox pointed out in his *History*, the terms of the truce were quite liberal.[11]   They also help substantiate a later verdict concerning Arran's leadership--that his government appeared determined to prove that the Protestants could avoid persecution only by slaughtering a cardinal and seizing a castle.[12]

The problem of St. Andrews Castle would not be solved by the Scottish governor alone.   He desperately needed help from outside quarters and the logical place to look for it was France, Scotland's partner in "the auld alliance."

Henry had come to terms with the king of France in the treaty of Campe on 7 June 1546.   The English were to keep Boulogne until 1554, restoring the fortifications there.   The French were to begin anew Henry's pension which had been stopped in 1535.   The Scots were to be comprehended in the accord.[13]

On 14 August the Scottish parliament devised a set of articles to be sent

---

[10]*State Papers*, 5:580-84, concerning the siege of St. Andrews, December 1546.

[11]Ibid., p. 582; Knox, *History*, 1:81.

[12]Ridley, *Knox*, p. 52.

[13]Elton, *Reform and Reformation*, p. 310; *Register*, 1:35, 1546; *Letters and Papers*, vol. 21, pt. 1:734, 14 August 1546.

to the French monarch and his ambassadors in England. Francis, they hoped, would do his best to help them secure their requests. The French king had insisted that Scotland be comprehended in the peace, and the Scots were most anxious to see Henry proclaim a peace with them on both sea and land.[14] The articles also contained a reference to the cardinal's murderers in which a request was made that the English king would not offer his assistance to them.[15]

Some three months later the Scottish privy council meeting in St. Andrews developed another list of requests for the king of France as it sought his help against Henry. Once again, Francis was to urge the English to keep the comprehension clause so that peace might prevail. Should Henry refuse to accept the article, Francis was urged to declare him an enemy in bold terms-- making himself master of the sea, as that was the best way to prevent an English invasion of either France or Scotland. The French king was also requested to send the Scots two hundred thousand crowns, ten thousand pikes, and twenty-four men who possessed military expertise in a variety of areas. These requests were to be sent with "all possible deligence" as the Scots believed that Henry's army intended to invade their kingdom in February. Concerning the governor, Francis was asked not to forget Arran's "pensioun and callaris of the ordour." The once vacillating governor's attachment to France was jarred little if at all by the death of his pro-French mentor, Cardinal Beaton.[16]

Arran's loyalty to Rome also suffered little, as his correspondence with

---

[14]Ibid., p. 729; *Acts of Parliaments*, 2:473.

[15]*Letters and Papers*, vol. 21, pt. 1:729, 14 August 1546; *Acts of the Parliaments*, 2:474.

[16]*Letters and Papers*, vol. 21, pt. 2:213, 26 November 1546; *Register*, 1:52-55, 26 November 1546.

Paul III and the cardinals indicates. According to Arran, Beaton's assassination in the castle which he held fortified for two years was abominable--"an unspeakable grief." The cardinal of St. Andrews had become for the governor ". . . a good and patriotic man, his near kinsman and confidant, whom he loved as a father."[17]

Arran proceeded to describe the events which had taken place since Beaton's murder, as well as the fear that Henry's army might capture St. Andrews Castle barely four hours from England by sea. If this occurred, the English would be able to threaten all of Fife, described as the most fertile of Scottish provinces. Arran also expressed fear for his son's safety, explaining that the latter had been kept by the cardinal for his better education--not as a hostage, which in truth he was. The governor's correspondence also revealed the belief that the murderers could not be taken by force, an impression proved false only after the intervention of the French.[18]

English assistance to these Castilians did not conform with the peace treaty signed between the English and the French which had comprehended the Scots.[19] Scottish dependence upon French mediaries to insure Henry's compliance with this aspect of the accord had failed. On 2 October 1546 the Scottish privy council decided to send its own commissioners to England. They were to offer their acceptance of the comprehension clause of the treaty of Campe and to secure an actual peace with Henry's realm. If the English king

---

[17]*Letters and Papers*, vol. 21 pt. 2:2, Arran to the pope and the cardinals, 1 September 1546.

[18]Ibid., pp. 2-3.

[19]Ibid., pp. 197-98, Selve to Paget, 18 November 1546.

failed to accept this embassy, one of the representatives was to travel to Francis seeking his protection should Henry make war against Scotland.[20]

The Scottish commissioners were David Paniter--the actual leader of the embassy--and Sir Adam Otterburn. There was a great deal of dissension among the leaders of the Scottish government at this time surrounding the mission.[21] Paniter, distrusted by both Mary of Guise and the French ambassador in Scotland, D'Oysel, was described as strictly the governor's tool. Paniter, it was suspected, carried with him secret instructions from Arran who solely commissioned him, to the deep regret of the dowager and the rest of the council.[22]

Regardless of Paniter's orders from the governor, the Scottish ambassadors' meetings with the English were stormy ones. Henry, in a fit of anger, told them that the comprehension clause had been granted upon Francis' request with conditions which the Scots had contravened by recent acts of piracy and hostility not only against the English but toward their allies, the Holy Roman Emperor's subjects, as well. Henry presented his case to the Scots in no uncertain terms. They were false people upon whom he would seek revenge.[23]

---

[20]Ibid., p. 103, 2 October 1546; *Register*, 1:43-44, 2 October 1546.

[21]*Letters and Papers*, vol. 21, pt. 2:185, Selve to the admiral of France, 10 November 1546; *Selve*, p. 55, Selve to the admiral of France, 10 November 1546.

[22]Ibid., pp. 53-55, Selve to Francis 1, 10 November 1546; *Letters and Papers*, vol. 21, pt. 2:185, Selve to Francis 1, 10 November 1546.

[23]Ibid., p. 197, Selve to Paget, 18 November 1546, p. 209, Selve to Francis 1, 25 November 1546, and pp. 217-18, Van Der Delft to Mary of Hungary, 29 November 1546; *Selve*, pp. 60-61, Selve to Francis 1, 25 November 1546; *Spanish Calendar*, 8:509-12, Van Der Delft to Mary of Hungary, 29 November 1546.

The Scots were disturbed by the king's conduct. Paniter reported to the French ambassador in London, Odet de Selve, that he thought that Henry was determined to renew his war with Scotland. Therefore, Paniter was anxious to revive French assistance. He pointed out that Francis could do greater damage to England by way of Scotland with two hundred thousand crowns than he could do by means of any other area for one million. Gunpowder was also desperately needed by the Scots. Francis could also take advantage of an Irish insurrection against the English, for the rebels daily solicited Arran's permission to utilize the Scottish islanders.[24]

The Scots had grown to know the English king well. In spite of their efforts to secure peace, they were preparing themselves for still another of Henry's major assaults. So suspicious were the English that they held the opinion that these "very cunning" Scottish commissioners were attempting to buy time and to sow distrust between England and the Empire.[25]

Nevertheless, a letter concerning these negotiations, written by Henry to Arran and the Scottish council on 20 December, a little over one month before his death, shows the strong perseverance with which he pursued his Scottish designs formulated in the wake of his victory at Solway Moss. Since the Scots had already failed to keep their promises regarding the Greenwich treaties, why should Henry have reason to negotiate once again with them? Nevertheless, the English king was so given to an honorable peace that such an understanding

---

[24]*Letters and Papers*, vol. 21, pt. 2:209, Selve to Francis 1, 25 November 1546; *Selve*, pp. 60-61, Selve to Francis 1, 25 November 1546.

[25]*Letters and Papers*, vol. 21, pt. 2:217-18, Van Der Delft to Mary of Hungary, 29 November 1546; *Spanish Calendar*, 8:512, Van Der Delft to Mary of Hungary, 29 November 1546.

with his northern neighbor was not impossible to achieve. Arran's government, however, would have to prove its sincerity by withdrawing its siege of St. Andrews until the future of those within it could be debated. Henry would interpret such a retreat as a "token of love and kindness." The English king recognized the occupants of the castle as adherents to his cause--particularly the marriage of Edward to Mary. Hence, his kingdom had favored them and had made promises to help them in whatever ways were necessary.[26]

Arran's government, as already shown, came to an understanding with the pro-English, Protestant band of assassins in the same month as Henry wrote his letter. Underlying the significance of the truce for this study is the fact that the governor's weakness, despite his protestations to the contrary, was profound. If his government were to survive, assistance must come from France.[27]

When the final showdown between the Scottish government and the occupants of St. Andrews Castle occurred during July 1547, Henry was dead. Unfortunately for the Scots, his kingdom's basic Scottish policy had changed hardly at all. Although his young son and successor, Edward VI, was never to rule with the iron fist of his father, the English government, like that of Scotland, was headed by a regent--the earl of Hertford, now the duke of Somerset.

Changes had occurred on the continent as well. Francis I had died only a few months after his great rival, the English king. He too was succeeded by a son, Henry II, inferior in strength to his father but nonetheless desirous of

---

[26]*State Papers*, 5:576-77, Henry 8 to the governor and the council of Scotland, 20 December 1546.

[27]*Letters and Papers*, vol. 21, pt. 2:xxxi and 295, 19 December 1546; *Register*, 1:57-58, 19 December 1546.

paying substantially more attention to Scotland.

Differences between the two new rulers, Somerset and Henry II, were obvious in their respective attitudes toward Scotland, particularly St. Andrews Castle. By July the incidents at the castle were to take on definite international implications. Scottish ties with the continent grew stronger as tension with England continued to mount.

In May 1547 Paniter finally reached the French court after having been delayed by the English with a memorial of eighteen articles of instruction from the Scottish governor. The first laid the basis for all the others. In short, Henry II was called upon to keep the Scots' comprehension clause in the latest treaty between England and France so that they might have a peace with their southern neighbor similar to that possessed by the French. The succeeding articles cited several English violations of the clause which were so great that Arran predicted in the course of time they would grow to outright conquest.[28]

Should this comprehension fail to be kept, it was hoped that France would send money and arms to its partner in "the auld alliance." If Henry II went so far as to land an army in England, the Scots would certainly cooperate from the north. The French king was also requested to gain the favor of Denmark and the Empire as well. Finally, Paniter was instructed to show the king that an absolution sent by Francis I to the assassins of Cardinal Beaton had not been enough to move them. Hence, Henry II should do what he could to

---

[28]Additional 33,531 folio 15, Mary Queen of Scots commission to David Paniter and John Hay, ambassadors to France seeking aid against Henry 8, countersigned by Arran, 24 January 1547; Additional 23,108 folio 8, Arran's instructions to Paniter, *c.* 1547; Additional 32,091 folio 140, Arran to Henry 2, 14 May 1547; Great Britain, *Historical Manuscripts Commission, Fifth Report of the Royal Commission on Historical Manuscripts, Part I, Report and Appendix* (London: Her Majesty's Stationery Office, 1876), p. 651.

secure a wider absolution from the pope.[29]

Preservation of an independent Scotland depended upon the kingdom's ties to the continent. The role of the pope had become a crucial one. The pro-English party wished to delay the papal absolution as long as possible so that the castle would remain in their hands for a longer period of time. They desired that the emperor intercede on their behalf in this regard with his friend the pope. But as the English stalled for time, the French party worked to expedite the absolution.[30]

The absolution that finally arrived from Rome during the spring, contained the phrase *Remittimus Irremissible*--"We remit the crime that can not be remitted. . . ." Hence, the terms of the truce were not kept and the castle was not surrendered. The Castilians had learned to play by their own rules, papal absolution or not. The Castilians' confident expectation of English aid justified this defiance.[31]

Surrender would have been to their advantage, however, for the French king acted decisively before the English protector--a sure prelude to later events within Scotland. On 29 June 1547 twenty-one French galleys with a large

---

[29]Ibid; Additional 23,108 folio 8, Arran's instructions to Paniter, *c.* 1547.

[30]*State Papers*, 5:583, concerning the siege of St. Andrews, December 1546; *Letters and Papers*, vol. 21, pt. 2:377-78, Dandino to Cardinal Farnese, 20 January 1547. On 26 April 1547, Arran wrote to Pope Paul 3 concerning punishments for Beaton's assassins, Additional 32,091 folio 140.

[31]Knox, *History*, 1:94-95; Great Britain, Public Record Office, *Calendar of the State Papers Relating to Scotland and Mary, Queen of Scots 1547-1603. Preserved in the Public Record Office, the British Museum, and Elsewhere in England*, Joseph Bain et al, eds. 13 vols. (Edinburgh: Her Majesty's General Register House, 1898-1969), vol. 1 (1547): February 1547, articles touching the castle of St. Andrews, pp. 1-2 and 2 April 1547, James Stewart of Cardonald to Wharton and Bischop, pp. 4-5. (Hereafter cited as *Scottish Calendar*.)

military force, ". . . the like whereof was never seen in the Firth before," arrived in sight of the beleaguered castle. At the same time, Arran was busy mustering an army which was described as "the starkest host and the monest, and wyth the best order" seen since Flodden.[32] According to English intelligence, the governor had never before commanded such a great army. Even though it was known that Arran was interested in taking Langholm, near the border, from the English, there was suspicion that he was up to something more important.[33]

Fulfilling the English expectations, the governor joined the French force in the siege of St. Andrews during the last week of July. The Castilians finally surrendered at the end of the month. Specifically, the occupants of the castle capitulated to the French, not to Arran nor to any other Scot who had ". . . traitorously betrayed them" by violating the December truce. The leaders of this band of insurgents were imprisoned in France while the lesser figures including John Knox, a latecomer to the castle, were sentenced to the French galleys until 1549. The castle itself was later ". . . razed to the ground, the block-houses thereof cast down, and the walls round about demolished." The Scots were moved in this action by the fact that such was the fate of places where cardinals were slain. They may also have feared that the English would recover the stronghold and use it to Scotland's detriment.[34]

The Castilians, who had defied Arran for fourteen months, had surrendered to the French after a siege of only five days and a bombardment of

---

[32]Ibid., p. 8, "Ye Wat Quha" to Wharton, 2 July 1547.

[33]Ibid., pp. 7-8, "Wait Quha" to Wharton, 28 June 1547.

[34]Knox., *History*, 1:95-98; Donaldson, *Scotland*, p. 76.

six hours.[35] This military capitulation was of greater significance than it appeared, for it indicated that if the governor were to continue leading his kingdom politically, he would have to do it with French assistance.

Somerset, on the other hand, clung to the idea of a dynastic marriage with the Scots.[36] His suggestion, however, that a peaceful solution might still be arranged with his northern neighbor was perhaps no more than a means of buying the English time. For Somerset's later actions proved that if the marriage were to take place, it would follow the roughest of wooing.[37]

The occupation of St. Andrews had never seemed as important to Somerset as it did to Henry II, who considered Scotland and English-held Boulogne to be the two main objectives of his foreign policy.[38] The protector, in the first place, was upset with the Castilians for having made the December truce without consulting the English government. Moreover, they had not sent Arran's son to the southern kingdom as had been previously requested of them by the English. As a result, in the summer of 1547, Somerset began to prepare a military campaign against the Scots, not anxious to change his overall strategy to assist the English agents in St. Andrews. The Castilians were to be utilized

---

[35]Ridley, *Knox*, p. 65.

[36]*Scottish Calendar*, 1:1-2, articles touching St. Andrews, February 1547, p. 2, articles by the Master of Rothes etc., February 1547, p. 2, Patrick Lord Gray to Edward 6 etc., 11 March 1547, p. 9, commission by Edward 6, 8 July 1547 which is important in that the Greenwich treaties are proven to be still very much alive, and pp. 9-10, instructions to the ambassadors, 18 July 1547.

[37]*Scottish Correspondence*, pp. 167 and 188-89, Otterburn to the queen dowager, 13 July 1547.

[38]Ibid., p. 166; Elton, *Reform and Reformation*, n. 340.

by him as only a diversion.[39]

Otterburn, the perceptive Scottish ambassador in London, saw the ominous character of Somerset's designs clearer than most. On 10 August he wrote to Arran describing events in the English capital. The protector as well as the lords of the council did not think that it was wise that the ambassador should remain in England during times of hostility unless he was empowered to negotiate an accord. Otterburn also relayed information on the extent of Somerset's preparations for a renewal of war. Another invasion of Scotland was imminent, for the English had been disturbed by the Scots' reoccupation of Langholm.[40]

Although it was certain that the invasion would soon take place, the appearance of a desire to resolve matters through negotiation was maintained by the protector. Somerset had reflected upon better ways to be followed than the "effusioun" of blood. He viewed himself as a man always given to peace and tranquility unless provoked to the contrary. Therefore, should Arran behave in a manner which would profit the wealth and commodity of both British realms, invasion could be avoided.[41] Nothing, however, came of this last minute effort of both sides to protect the commonwealth of the two realms or to prevent the shedding of Christian blood.[42]

---

[39]Ridley, *Knox*, p. 60; *Scottish Calendar*, 1:11, Somerset to Warwick, August 1547 and passim pp. 12-19.

[40]*Scottish Correspondence*, p. 192, Otterburn to the governor, 10 August 1547.

[41]Ibid., p. 193.

[42]Ibid., pp. 193-194 and 168; *Scottish Calendar*, 1:15-16, Somerset to Sir Adam Otterburn, August 1547.

Arran's government busily prepared for the impending invasion. Reports to the English indicated, nevertheless, that the governor had difficulty in securing recruits.[43]   Glencairn, once again in the service of the English, reported that Arran had summoned every man between the ages of sixteen and sixty to muster at Fala Moor on the last of August with victuals for twenty days. Few had heeded his call. According to Glencairn, Somerset and his army would have little trouble during the invasion, for the governor was reported to fear his own people more than the English.[44]

Amidst such reports, the English launched their invasion in September.[45] The most important aspect of this--the third of Somerset's major assaults upon the Scots--was his victory at Pinkiecleuch, near Musselburgh on Black Saturday, 10 September. The trouble that Arran had reportedly encountered in mustering troops was overcome. The Scots met the protector's army, numbering from fifteen to sixteen thousand, with a force that was estimated as high as almost thirty thousand. Nonetheless, these numbers were a poor substitute for superior English equipment and cavalry. What numerical confidence the Scots enjoyed failed to serve their interests as they repeated some of the same mistakes which they had made at Flodden. They allowed themselves to be drawn from an advantageous position, were attacked while in disorder, and were routed in a tremendous slaughter of thousands caught between the Esk and the sea.[46]

---

[43]Ibid., pp. 17-18, laird of Ormistown to Somerset, 2 September 1547.

[44]Ibid., pp. 18-19, enclosure of Glencairn to Lennox and Wharton, 6 September 1547.

[45]Ibid., pp. 19-20, Lennox and Wharton to Somerset, 16 September 1547.

[46]*Complaynt of Scotlande*, xiv; Knox, *History*, 1:98-101; Donaldson, *Scotland*, pp. 76-77; *Scottish Correspondence*, p. 168; Ridley, *Knox*, p. 65; *Patten's Expedition into Scotland* in

The battle of Pinkie, the last major battle between Scotland and England as separate nations, was a milestone in the history of Anglo-Scottish relations.[47] The battle ranked with both Flodden Field and Solway Moss as yet another humiliating defeat of the Scots.[48]

Somerset withdrew from Scotland following his victory, but the Anglo-Scottish war continued. The English maintained their traditional pattern of ravaging the borders, adding to this destruction a new strategy as well. The success of the Castilians in holding St. Andrews Castle convinced the English of the feasibility of occupying Scottish strongholds to further their cause. For varying periods from the latter part of 1547 to the summer of 1549, English garrisons possessed Inchcolm, Broughty Castle, Inchkeith, Dundee, and Haddington. Hence, they were able to dominate both the Forth and Tay estuaries as well as to terrorize the Scots from the Lothian countryside to Edinburgh.[49]

John Knox reported that most of the Lothian area from Edinburgh eastward was either won to the English cause or destroyed. Lord Methven, a frequent correspondent with the queen dowager, maintained that there were four principal reasons behind the temporary successes of the English over the Scots. They were: reformist ideas, the fear of the English and the subsequent desire

---

Tudor Tracts, pp. 53-157; Beer, *Northumberland*, pp. 61-65.

[47]*Tudor Tracts*, p. 107.

[48]*Complaynt of Scotlande*, xiv.

[49]M. L. Bush, *The Government Policy of Protector Somerset* (Montreal: McGill-Queen's University Press, 1975) devotes a large segment of his work to the evaluation of these garrisons; Donaldson, *Scotland*, p. 76; Ellis, *Original Letters*, first series, 2:148-9, "King Edward the Sixth, to the Duke of Somerset, upon his Successes against the Scotch," 18 September 1547.

for safety, the want of particular profits, and the yearning for more quietness and justice.[50]

In short, the English enjoyed a temporary success by exploiting Arran's weaknesses, making assurances, and harvesting reformist opinions sowed during Henry VIII's reign within his neighbor's soil. Somerset also benefited from the assistance of pro-English tracts which pointed out the advantages of the "godly pretence" or "purpose" to unite the two British kingdoms first formulated by Henry VIII--now inherited by his erstwhile lieutenant. According to the confident protector, ". . . for avoydeng confusion of names, both the realmes thus united, shal bere the name of Grete Britayn which is no newe name but thold name to them booth."[51]

Scottish resistance to such plans, however, was not dead. The long history of rivalry between the two British kingdoms had repeatedly pointed to the fact that force was hardly the best way to achieve English goals in regard to Scotland. Henry VIII was aware of this lesson of history--hence his scheme of wooing to subvert Scottish independence soon after his victory at Solway Moss. But regardless of the tactics employed by the English, Scotland was insured by its partner in "the auld alliance."

By the end of 1547 there were reports of both French men and money

---

[50]Donaldson, *Scotland*, pp. 76-78; Knox, *History*, 1:101; *Scottish Correspondence*, pp. 240-43, Methven to the queen dowager, 3 June 1548; also see Merriman, "The Assured Scots."

[51]*Scottish Calendar*, 1:87-88, instructions for John Brende on the assurance of the earl of Argyle, February 1548; Donaldson, *Scotland*, pp. 77-78; the following works are found in *Complaynt of Scotlande*: *The Exhortacion of James Harrysone, Scottisheman*, 1547, pp. 207-36, *The Epistle of the Lord Protector Somerset*, 1548, pp. 237-46, *The Epitome of Nicholas Bodrugan alias Adams*, 1548, pp. 247-56. *Cf.* with *Scottish Calendar*, 1:141-45, "Extracts of the Godly and Golden Book, etc.," 9 July 1548 and pp. 180-81, James Henrison to Somerset, 1549.

ready to serve Scottish interests during the coming months. In February 1548, the northern kingdom scored one of its greatest victories of the period from late 1547 to the summer of 1549. The Scots repulsed an English offensive attempt of Lennox and Thomas Wharton, a deputy warden, at Dumfries. Although not a great military achievement, it did have special significance, as it lifted the Scots' morale and thereby strengthened their attempts to dislodge the entrenched English.[52]

Also near the end of February, Arran was able to take Saltoun ". . . quhair he had hangit all that he fand in it. The rest of the howsis, herand that he had done swa, send to hym all the kies of the strenthis" which had been taken by Lord Grey of Wilton, the English lieutenant on the borders, during his most recent attack.[53]

Nevertheless, Arran needed more than victories of this sort if he were to continue to lead the nation which had been so divided by the destruction of Pinkie. Somerset might never be able to gain possession of the young queen of Scots or to secure his king's "godly purpose" of uniting the two realms into a truly Great Britain, but he had the ability to inflict further damage and destruction upon the Scots who stubbornly resisted English demands. Arran quite clearly realized this and saw the importance of forcing the English out of his kingdom or at least, coming to terms with them. For a time, the latter

---

[52]*Scottish Correspondence*, p. 197; *Scottish Calendar*, 1:55-56, Sir Ralph Bulmer to Somerset, 30 December 1547, p. 57, enclosure of anonymous letter to Lord Gray of Scotland, 3 January 1548 and p. 57, Grey of Wilton to Somerset, 5 January 1548; Donaldson, *Scotland*, p. 76.

[53]*Scottish Correspondence*, pp. 219-20, John Erskine to the queen dowager, March 1548; *Scottish Calendar*, 1:88-89, Grey of Wilton to Somerset, 1 March 1548 and p. 89, Grey of Wilton to Somerset, 6 March 1548.

alternative seemed the more appealing, for the governor was disappointed that certain French support promised him had failed to materialize.[54]

Thus, during March 1548, Arran showed a willingness to negotiate with the English through the use of Huntly, the Scottish chancellor, who had been captured at Pinkie. Huntly had placed the blame for Scotland's defeat upon the "over-precipitancy" of Arran "in forcing an engagement." Had the governor followed Huntly's advice "to temporise a little"--an approach once so successfully followed by him--the Scots could have perhaps achieved a "sure victory," so the chancellor thought.[55]

Yet, as a result of this failure, Huntly found himself in a position of great importance, not totally unlike that of Henry VIII's Solway prisoners. A major aspect of his negotiations centered around an exchange of Scottish prisoners for the men taken at St. Andrews, provided the French king cooperated by sending them. Arran had ordered a meeting of his secret council on 10 April to make arrangements concerning this peace initiative.[56]

The motive behind this appeal for peace has been questioned. It has been contended that an anonymous letter written to John Hamilton, the abbot of Paisley and bastard brother of the governor, provides a ". . . sinister suspicion that the secret intelligence of the enemy was imparted from no patriotic motive, and that the informant and the recipient were working hand in glove." The letter was probably written by an adherent of the Hamilton faction who was an

---

[54]Ibid.

[55]*Scottish Correspondence*, 241-42 footnote 3.

[56]*Scottish Calendar*, 1:104, Huntly to Somerset, 29 March 1548 and pp. 104-5, the governor to Huntly, 26 March 1548.

English agent as well at a time when Arran was willing to reach a settlement with Somerset.[57]

Paisley and even the governor himself were clearly doing whatever they could to enhance the welfare of their family from securing ecclesiastical offices to pensions of various kinds.[58] But whatever truth there is to the contention concerning the abbot's motives in the negotiating process, Arran's government did not come to terms with the English.

The apparent attempt of the governor to follow an independent course of action between the pro-English and the extreme pro-French faction led by Mary of Guise, who had recently reaped the benefits of her family's close association with Henry II, did not materialize. Arran, nevertheless, continued to nourish the idea of keeping the young queen in Scotland and marrying her to his son. His unwillingness to agree to the terms demanded by the English concerning the long sought marriage of the two sovereigns is illustrated quite well in a report of Grey to Somerset which described Paisley as coming to Berwick commissioned to negotiate peace, while Arran stood "stiffly" against the English, primarily in hopes of marrying his son to the young Queen.[59] This report mentioned, however, that Huntly thought Arran might relinquish this hope and become more inclined to English interests if upon meeting the abbot, he could produce a letter from the queen dowager which showed how she abused the

---

[57]*Scottish Correspondence*, pp. 200, 220-23, ? to John Hamilton, 15 March 1548 and footnote 5 on pp. 222-23.

[58]Donaldson, *Scotland*, p. 77.

[59]*Scottish Calendar*, 1:107 number 218, Grey of Wilton to Somerset 3 April 1548.

governor with dalliance, never intending to do what he expected.[60]
Nevertheless, this attempt at reconciliation was doomed from the start by the
designs of a much more powerful nation than either of the two island kingdoms-
-France--where the queen dowager's influence prevailed.

To think that Henry II would condone a Scottish settlement with the
English before he had achieved his own goals in regard to Arran's kingdom was
absurd. Not the least of these goals was possession of the young queen of Scots
and the major strongholds located there--desires not unlike those of an earlier
English monarch named Henry.[61] Although additional French assistance was
a necessity for the Scots should warfare continue, Arran was disturbed by the
conditions upon which Henry II was willing to grant it. These terms included
possession of his son as well as the castles of Edinburgh, Dumbarton, and
Dunbar, to say nothing of the young queen. Nevertheless, the governor cast his
lot with the French by agreeing to these demands. By this time, the French king
had learned how to deal with Arran. Security must be obtained if the necessary
aid was to be given.[62]

Hence, the feeble efforts of the house of Hamilton to steer an
independent course of action in Scottish politics during 1548 ended when the
French arrived. In June, Arran stood firmly committed to the French cause.[63]

---

[60]Ibid.

[61]Ibid., 37, laird of Longniddry to Somerset, 5 November 1547.

[62]Ibid., p. 111, Grey of Wilton to Somerset, 28 April 1548.

[63]Scottish Correspondence, p. 201; Scottish Calendar, 1:119, Grey of Wilton to Somerset,
12 June 1548, pp. 120-21, Grey of Wilton to Somerset, 16 June 1548, p. 122 number 250, Grey
of Wilton to Somerset, 18 June 1548 or pp. 119-33 passim for French activity in Scotland
during June 1548.

Scotland received its aid; France received its security. Most importantly, however, for this study, the pro-French party headed by Mary of Guise had triumphed over Arran. Only a short time would pass before that victory would be evident in Scottish politics.

French guns, therefore, did more than shatter the delusions of the house of Hamilton. The cherished dreams which Henry VIII and Somerset had nurtured were dealt a death blow by this direct, massive intervention of Henry II's government.

A state of warfare would continue to exist between "the auld enemy" and the partners in "the auld alliance" until March 1550. Then the treaty of Boulogne signed between the French and the English fully comprehended the Scots. France immediately recovered the town for which the treaty was named; England received merely half of the compensation agreed to at Campe; and the remainder of the English troops were to withdraw from Scotland.[64]

Thus the fate of the English marriage, the union of the two island kingdoms, and the destiny of Arran as governor of Scotland were sealed. The English rough wooing had succeeded in so far as it led to the total capitulation of Scotland to France and the marriage of the young Queen Mary to the dauphin--the future Francis II. This was hardly the result intended by Henry VIII, Protector Somerset, and their not always trustworthy but seemingly essential band of assured Scots.

---

[64]Egerton 1818 folios 4, 5, and 6, Arran's instructions concerning defenses, 27 August 1548; *Foedera*, 15:211 for the treaty of Boulogne; Ferguson, *Relations*, pp. 62-63; Elton, *Reform and Reformation*, pp. 359-60.

CHAPTER IX

The Triumph of France and the End of Arran's Regency

The reasons behind Scotland's capitulation to France in the summer of 1548 actually took shape much earlier in that year. As early as January, Arran had come to a basic understanding with Henry II. Despite an apparent willingness to negotiate with the English, the governor was making overtures to the French. In November 1547, it was reported that the queen dowager, upon Arran's advice, had written an urgent letter to France seeking immediate assistance against the English. So desperate was the situation in Scotland that the Scottish council wanted to take the church's jewels and chalices in order to support the war. The kirkmen also feared that an attempt would be made to get their temporal lands.[1]

Amidst such circumstances later in the month, Seigneur D'Oysel, the French ambassador in Scotland, departed for France. He would ". . . ask pay for 3000 horse, and 12,000 foot, which if his King gives, the strengths of Scotland, and the princess to be at his pleasure."[2]

---

[1]*Scottish Calendar*, 1:41, Nynian Cockburn's report, 17 November 1547.

[2]Ibid., p. 42, Grey of Wilton to Somerset, 24 November 1547.

If French help were not given, the Scots alone would have to do what they could against their foes. Talk of the governor's incompetency and diminishing popularity abounded. For example, some believed that should Scotland again confront England, Arran ". . . for his greatness must not dismount, but if he should remain mounted, the rest might fly: therefore he must appoint a lieutenant, and himself not come to the field."[3] Fortunately, Arran realized his own limitations and the crucial dilemma of the Scots. He saw the need for his nation to have stronger leadership than that which he and his bastard brother were capable of giving. Even his attempt to negotiate with the English in April depended on whether or not the French king would cooperate with him in the exchange of some of the Castilians. Arran's hands were tied.

It was hoped, therefore, that D'Oysel's mission would lead to important results. Henry II and his council kept the ambassador in close consultation for three days as they discussed the help which was "demanded" by "poor deserted Scotland."[4] Probably, D'Oysel played a significant role in the contract framed between Arran and the French king on 27 January 1548. In it, the governor promised to help gain the consent of his parliament for the marriage of the young queen to the dauphin, her removal to France, and the transfer of some important Scottish strongholds to French hands, in return for the title of a rich French duchy.[5]

---

[3]Ibid.

[4]*Spanish Calendar*, 9:216-17, Jean of St. Mauris to the queen dowager of Hungary, November 1547.

[5]*Scottish Correspondence*, pp. 224-25; Knox, *History*, 1:102; David Hay Fleming, *Mary Queen of Scots from Her Birth to Her Flight into England: A Brief Biography: With Critical Notes, a Few Documents Hitherto Unpublished, and an Itinerary* (London: Hodder and Stroughton, 1898), pp. 193-94 footnote 83.

By June 1548, however, only one of the three strongholds previously mentioned--Dunbar--was placed under the control of the French. Both Dumbarton and Edinburgh were kept. The latter, according to the governor, would be held until Haddington had been assaulted and the former, according to Knox, until the question concerning the possession of Mary could be settled.[6]

Not until February 1549, did Arran actually become the duke of Châtelherault, thus gaining a duchy worth twelve thousand livres per year. His half-brother by this time had finally been appointed Beaton's successor at the archbishopric of St. Andrews. The governor, together with Huntly, Argyle, and Angus, each of whom had served the English in one way or another, was also taken into the order of the Cockle, or St. Michael. In June 1549, the French king entered into a bond with Arran which recognized the governor's right to the crown should Mary die childless.[7]

Even before Arran's formal confirmation as duke, Henry II had flattered the governor on 28 April 1548 by consenting that during Queen Mary's minority, he should have a free hand in the disposal of all Scottish affairs. Because of the governor's ". . . diligence, and the loss sustained by him in the Queen's service," Henry assured him of a full discharge of financial responsibility upon her majority. Should the young Mary attempt to do anything against Arran's authority, she would be restrained. But before these concessions were enumerated, a preamble stated that they resulted from the fact that Arran

---

[6]*Scottish Calendar*, 1:125-26, Grey of Wilton to Somerset, 23 June 1548 and pp. 146-47, Palmer and Holcroft to Somerset, 13 July 1548; Knox, *History*, 1:102-3.

[7]Sloane 3199 folio 243, bond of Henry 2 with Arran, 7 June 1549; also, Additional 10,012 for a letter from Henry 2 in 1549 supporting Châtelherault's claim to the Scottish throne; Knox *History*, 1:102-3; Donaldson, *Scotland*, pp. 78-80, *Cf.* with *State Papers*, 5:460, which indicates that Angus had much earlier been taken into the order of the Cockle.

had agreed to send his sovereign to France for her greater protection against such attempts as those made by Edward VI during the past year to gain possession of the young Scottish queen.[8]

On the same day, Henry II also promised Arran that the young Hamilton would marry Mlle. de Montpensier, the oldest daughter of the duke of Montpensier, as soon as both were nubile. This promise was supposedly made in reward for the governor's services to Francis I and in anticipation of strengthening the friendship and alliance between Scotland and France.[9] In truth, it was a consolation for the abandonment of the governor's dream to secure Mary's hand for his own son. This arrangement was also part of the French king's plan to secure a satisfactory pledge for what had proved to be in the past, the governor's untrustworthy word.

History had repeated itself for Arran. Two kings both named Henry, one in 1543 and the other five years later, had attempted to woo the young Hamilton in hopes of gaining possession of the young queen of Scotland and marrying her to their respective heirs. Whereas one king failed abysmally, the other succeeded triumphantly. Above all, the ultimate aims of both Tudor and Valois were basically the same. Each hoped to subordinate Scotland to his own particular kingdom. The danger, however, of Scottish absorption into France was mild compared to the alternative.

In late spring, the Hamilton heir was transferred to France as a token of

---

[8]*Historical Manuscripts Commission, Eleventh Report*, p. 39.

[9]Marguerite Wood, ed., *Foreign Correspondence with Marie de Lorraine, Queen of Scotland, from the Originals in the Balcarres Papers, 1537-1557*, Scottish Historical Society Publications, third series, vols. 4 and 7 (Edinburgh: University Press, 1923-25), 4:197-98, copy of the king of France's promise concerning the earl of Arran's son, 18 April 1548. (Hereafter cited as *Balcarres Papers*.)

his father's good faith in regard to Henry II.[10] The life of this child in captivity, first as a hostage of Beaton, then the Castilians, and now the king of France, helps account for the mental illness which plagued him in his later life--a living nightmare resulting in no small part from his father's vacillation as a governor of a kingdom ridden by division, distrust, and deceit.

By early June, Arran himself, in spite of all types of French assurances, was in a state of deep despair:

> I hear from Edinburgh that the Governor is so grieved at the spoil and devasting of Dalkeith, "passyoned" by his unadvised rendering of Dunbarton to the Queen, "tormented" at his son's delivery to France, his estimation abated, his vain expectation at an end, the French aid so slow, some say gone back, that he had thrown himself into a sharp sickness and lies at the point of death.[11]

Even the queen dowager was disturbed by the delay of her native country. Yet, as French aid revived in late June, so too did the governor. Thereupon, events transpired quickly.

A new Franco-Scottish force focused its attention upon Haddington, garrisoned by the English who believed that keeping Haddington meant winning Scotland.[12] The problem of Haddington continued to be a major concern of the Scots until September 1549, when the English finally abandoned it as a result

---

[10]*Spanish Calendar*, 9:269, Van der Delft to Charles 5, 25 May 1548.

[11]*Scottish Calendar*, 1:116-17, Grey of Wilton to Somerset, 7 June 1548.

[12]Ibid., p. 131, Grey of Wilton to Somerset, 28 June 1548.

of French attacks on their stronghold in Boulogne.[13]

Meanwhile, within a very short time after the arrival of this major French assistance, the Scottish parliament convened on 7 July 1548 at the abbey at Haddington and gave official recognition to those agreements made earlier in the year between Arran and the French king. It was certainly much easier to come to terms with the French than it had been with the English during 1543. At the meeting, Dessé, the French commander at Haddington, acting in the position of ambassador extraordinary, read a letter of Henry II stating that in view of Scotland's war with England, the king was firmly committed to "the auld alliance." Hence, Henry would do nothing less than ". . . aide support manteine and defend at his powar" the whole Scottish realm. He would give his brotherly help--not by words but by deed--against all who would attempt to harm that kingdom. The French navy and army had directions to restore Scotland's traditional liberties and privileges, as well as to recover all strongholds from the enemy. This was to be done with the advice and assistance of Arran and the Scottish nobility. In addition to the present French military assistance, a promise was made to send whatever was needed in the form of additional men, munitions, or money to repress the English during the war and to preserve Scotland's liberties and freedom from them and all others.[14]

Thereupon, Arran, in the Queen of Scots' name, ratified and approved with the consent of the Scottish estates the marriage of Mary with the dauphin. This marriage was granted upon the condition that the king would continue to defend Scotland's laws and liberties as if they were those of France. In

---

[13]Ibid., pp. 178-80, Thomas Fisher to William Cecil, 17 September 1549; Donaldson, *Scotland*, p. 79; *Accounts of the Treasurer*, 9:341.

[14]*Acts of the Parliaments*, 2:481-82.

addition, the Scottish queen would be married to no one other than the king's son.[15]

What Henry VIII had tried so desperately to achieve was accomplished easily by the French king with the help of generous financial inducements for the frequently wavering Scottish nobility who feared English encroachment.[16] In late July, the young queen departed on a French ship. She arrived in France in mid-August--a glorious triumph for the pro-French party in Scottish politics.[17]

Quite clearly, Mary of Guise, Arran's major rival within the faction-ridden Scottish government, had taken full advantage of the governor's predicament. Since the death of Beaton, Arran had been faced with enormous problems, not the least of which was Scottish disunity and the subversion of authority--factors which had contributed to the disaster at Pinkie.[18]

The capitulation of the Scots, particularly Arran, to Henry II, enhanced the queen dowager's position because her family enjoyed a close affinity with the French crown.[19] By exerting continuous pressure upon the Scots, Mary of Guise built for herself a powerful and prestigious party from those individuals whom Arran had alienated by judicial fines, nepotism, avarice, and political

---

[15]Ibid.

[16]*Scottish Calendar*, 1:132-33, Grey of Wilton to Somerset, 30 June 1548.

[17]W. M. Bryce, "Mary Stuart's Voyage to France in 1548," *English Historical Review* 22 (January 1907):43-50.

[18]Henderson, *Mary Queen of Scots*, 1:89-90, *Scottish Correspondence*, pp. 240-43, Methven to the queen dowager, 3 June 1548.

[19]Ibid., pp. 179-81, Otterburn to the queen dowager, April 1547 and pp. 182-83, Earl Marischal to the queen dowager, 2 May 1547.

incompetence.[20]

The weakness of Arran in the political affairs of Scotland is well exemplified in a letter to the dowager on 7 October 1552, in which he anxiously looked for an answer from her concerning state matters. In particular, the site where the council was to meet posed a problem for the governor. He would not choose a location until he knew that it satisfied her.[21]

The irony of this episode in Anglo-Scottish relations is, that just when "the auld enemy" was being turned away, "the auld ally" took on many of the same attributes as the Scots' neighbor to the south. There had been numerous disagreements between the Scots and their French allies almost from the start of their assistance in June 1548. In November of that year an English report pictured Scotland torn not only from without but from within as well:

> The country is so wasted there is nothing to destroy. The bareness, want of lodging, scarcity, wet, and cold, makes war here more painful than elsewhere, wastes men and horses, brings men out of heart, causing even them to forswear war, that cannot live without it. Yet you above, that judge our doings, weigh our pain, and not always our success. You think we have done little, yet we know we have travailed much. The enemy, though full of variance and suspicion among themselves, always agree against us. The Governor is "as one that holdeth the wolf by the eares, in doubt to holde, and in daunger to let goo."[22]

---

[20]Ibid., pp. 325 and 335.

[21]Ibid., pp. 334 and 360-61, the governor to the queen dowager, 7 October 1552.

[22]*Scottish Calendar*, 1:169, Brende to Sir John Mason, 29 November 1548; Ellis, *Original Letters*, third series, 3:291-300, "Thomas Fisher to the Duke of Somerset, Protector, apprizing him of Intelligence he had received concerning tumults at Edinburgh; and of hostilities committed by the French and Almains," 12 October 1548.

All was not harmony between Scotland and France. In 1550 following the treaty of Boulogne, Henry II wrote to the French ambassador in Constantinople giving further credence to the idea that "the auld ally" had much more in mind than unselfish support for its downtrodden friend:

> . . . By making this aforesaid peace, I have pacified the kingdom of Scotland that I hold and possess with such command and obedience such as I have in France, to which kingdoms I have joined and united another, which is England, which by a perpetual peace, union, alliance and confederation, I am able to dispose of as my very own, the king, and the subjects and its powers: so that the said three kingdoms together are now able to be considered a single monarchy.[23]

Henry II had solved the so-called "British Problem" by transforming Scotland into a mere appendage of France, and England into a position of clientage.[24] This ambitious French monarch had plans of incorporating Ireland as well, thereby providing a truly comprehensive solution to the problems existing in the isles to his north.[25]

In view of such, Arran's tenure in office became little else than a

---

[23]Quoted in Gladys Dickinson, "Instructions to the French Ambassador, 30 March 1550," *Scottish Historical Review* 26 (1947): 155-56. (Hereafter cited as Dickinson, "Instructions.") This is a translation of:
> . . . En faisant ladite paix, j'ai pacifié le royaume d'Escosse, que je tiens et possède avec tel commandement et obéissance que j'ay en France, auxquels deux royaumes j'en ay joint et uny un autre, qui est L'Angleterre, dont par une paix perpetuelle, union, alliance et confédération, je puis disposer, comme de moi-mesme, du roy, et des sujets et de ses facultez: de sorte que lesdits trois royaumes ensemble se peuvent maintenant estimer une mesme monarchie.

[24]Ferguson, *Relations*, p. 63.

[25]Dickinson, "Instructions," p. 156.

camouflage. The report of an English informer named Matthew Strick in 1551 stated that D'Oysel had almost sovereign authority in political and judicial concerns--having his own provost who arrested and executed criminals.[26] Nevertheless, there was also the belief that the governor's bastard brother, now the archbishop of St. Andrews, appeared to be "the most influential man in the kingdom."[27] Regardless, French domination of Scotland could not be denied. Many Scotsmen disliked this influence so strongly that it was believed that more Frenchmen would be needed to subdue the natives. Although most French soldiers had been recalled home, some remained at the fortresses. Strick's report suggested that if the French gained Dumbarton and Edinburgh Castles in addition to those they already had, ". . . they would be masters of the country." A bulwark with the arms of France carved upon it had already been erected before the gate of Edinburgh Castle.[28]

Arran's camouflage failed to conceal the French influence not only in the internal affairs of Scotland but in its diplomatic affairs as well. Problems which had plagued the Scots for years on the continent were officially brought to an end when the treaty of Binche was signed with the Holy Roman Empire in late 1550. Mary of Guise played a significant role in gaining support for it.[29]

---

[26]Donaldson, *Scotland*, p. 81; *Spanish Calendar*, 10:339, report of Matthew Strick, July ? 1551.

[27]Ibid.

[28]Ibid., p. 340.

[29]*Scottish Calendar*, 1:184, Charles 5 and the queen of Scots, 1 April 1551; *Register*, 1:89, 22 April 1550; *Spanish Calendar*, 10:174, commission of Erskine to conclude a truce or peace with the emperor, the queen dowager of Hungary, or their delegates, 8 September 1550, p. 197, queen dowager of Hungary to the council of state, 19 December 1550, and p. 339, report of Matthew Strick, July ? 1551.

The French influence once again manifested itself when matters of a more urgent sort were officially settled with the English. The French envoy, M. de Lansac, was present when the Scots chosen from Mary of Guise's followers finally signed the treaty of Norham on 10 June 1551.

By this time, Somerset had also fallen from power and was replaced by the duke of Northumberland. The new regent spared Somerset the agony of accepting the treaty of Angers on 19 July 1551. This accord with France was an open admission of the failure of his and Henry VIII's Scottish policy. In it, Edward VI was betrothed to a French princess instead of the coveted Scottish queen. Northumberland's unpleasant task was to govern a kingdom which had little choice but to submit to France in hopes that a renewal of the traditional rivalry between Hapsburg and Valois would allow the Tudors time to regain their strength.[30]

Not even the strong influence of Arran's bastard brother could do much to alter the entrenchment of France and its bequest, the queen dowager, in the northern kingdom. As the political influence of Arran and his family waned, the profits of the house of Hamilton waxed.[31] Even the remote possibility of Arran seeking assistance from his old rival, the king of England, on the basis of a new religion failed to materialize and help his foundering position within the political

---

[30]Elton, *Reform and Reformation*, pp. 359-60; Beer, *Northumberland*, p. 113; *Scottish Correspondence*, pp. 327 and 349-51, Maxwell to the queen dowager, 14 June 1551; *Scottish Calendar*, 1:186, treaty of peace between Edward 6 and Mary Queen of Scots, 10 June 1551; *Foedera*, 15:265.

[31]*Scottish Correspondence*, pp. 329-30; Donaldson, *Scotland*, pp. 81-83; R. K. Hannay, Jane Harvey, and Marguerite Woods, "Some Papal Bulls among the Hamilton Papers," *Scottish Historical Review* 22 (1924):40-41.

structure of Scotland.[32]   In 1553, the Catholic Mary Tudor succeeded her
Protestant half-brother, negating the chances of another such appeal to the
southern kingdom.

In 1554 events finally came to a head for Arran. What had been all but
an official fact for the past few years--his surrender of power as regent of
Scotland to the stronger personality of Mary of Guise--came to legal fruition.
Without the support of the archbishop of St. Andrews, who was sick and unable
to speak, and having received a satisfactory and lucrative settlement for himself
and his family with the consent of the queen dowager--he resigned his office.[33]

The Scottish parliament of April 1554 officially recognized this transfer
of power.[34] By this time, however, the author of the fittingly titled *Diurnal of
Remarkable Occurents* could report the sombre news that all the lords opposed
the man who had struggled to lead their nation during a most important period
of their history--a quiet ending to a most hectic regency.[35]

---

[32]Ibid., *Spanish Calendar*, 11:41-42, advice sent by Jehan Scheyfve, 13 May 1553;
Donaldson, *Scotland*, p. 83.

[33]*Historical Manuscripts Commission, Eleventh Report*, pp. 40-41; *Balcarres Papers*, 7:245-
48, bishop of Ross to the dowager, 1 October 1554 and pp. 256-58, bishop of Ross to ?, 31
October 1554 on the marriage of the governor's son; Henderson, *Mary Queen of Scots*, 1:90.

[34]*Acts of the Parliaments*, 2:600-4.

[35]*Diurnal*, p. 51.

CHAPTER X

Conclusion

James Hamilton, second earl of Arran and governor of Scotland from 1543 until 1554, holds a distinctive position in the long and turbulent history of Anglo-Scottish relations.   Because of his birthright and claim to be second person in the realm, the problems of state were placed in his hands in early January 1543, during a most trying period of his kingdom's history.   Only weeks before, the English had gained one of their greatest victories over the Scots at the battle of Solway Moss.   Soon thereafter came the death of their king, James V, who left a week-old infant, Mary Queen of Scots, to rule this troubled land.

Battlefield defeats and royal minorities were not new to Scotland--they were old problems whose severity, nonetheless, was not lessened by past experience.   But for the Scots, the year 1543 held much more than merely meeting the challenge once again of these two historical experiences.   A new ingredient had compounded their dilemma.   The Scots' neighbor to the south, Henry VIII, had formulated during December 1542 an ingenious diplomatic scheme intended to undermine the independence of their kingdom.   Force was forsaken for the belief that cunning could somehow succeed where military might had always failed. A marriage treaty and a perpetual peace between the two British kingdoms would provide the opportunity whereby Henry could gain personal possession of the young Scottish queen and ultimately subvert her nation's sovereignty. Obvious impediments, however, lay in the English king's path of success, not the least of which was the earl of Arran.

British historians have been generally unsympathetic to this young Scottish leader who shouldered the responsibility of leading his nation through this unenviable situation. A closer examination of his regency, however, brings this traditional view into question. The fact that Arran possessed personal qualities not always becoming to a great leader does not at all diminish his importance and ultimate success in thwarting the Scottish policy of his nemesis, Henry VIII.

Interestingly enough, it was the governor's apparent weaknesses which did so much to convince Henry and his friends that Arran would be an ideal catspaw whereby the English dream of ruling Scotland could be realized. Arran's pro-English proclivities, particularly in regard to religious reform and his close association with the Douglases and others of the king's party, also convinced Henry of the feasibility of his dream. Such an attitude did much to discredit the king's policy of 1543, making it appear naive and inept in the extreme.

The governor's reputation within his kingdom was also tarnished by what appeared to many Scots to be too close an association with this pro-English party and Henry's foolish policy. By steadfastly pursuing his ultimate goal--an independent Scotland's peaceful co-existence with England based upon the Greenwich treaties--Arran incurred the wrath of many of his contemporaries who earnestly questioned his political loyalties. To many a Scot, particularly those in Beaton's pro-French camp, Arran was none other than a heretic and a good Englishman determined to sell Scotland to Henry.

These Scots could not see the governor's true motives, for out of his obvious weaknesses emerged an unwillingness to act any way other than verbally. Although one nineteenth-century historian contended that Arran: ". . . captivated the hearts and inspired the hopes of the best and most enlightened of his countrymen, by devising liberal measures and lending his powerful influence to the friends of peace and evangelical religion," he did not possess "the strength and courage of the true soldier."[1] By using "fare wordes and promyses" the vacillating governor pursued a quiet but nonetheless, consistent temporizing policy with the English king which for a time preserved an indispensable peace with his realm. For example, in the early summer of 1543, as Henry's scheme became generally known, Arran admitted to his council that obviously Scotland was not able to resist the English. Hence, "by fare wordes and promyses" made in the Greenwich treaties, the Scots would be able to defer the threat from their southern neighbor until a time when they could resist more successfully. In addition, throughout the first eight and in many respects, most important months of his regency, Arran continually delayed moving against his and the English king's enemies, chief of whom was David Beaton. Excluding the cardinal's initial arrest, a secure peace was consistently cited as the prerequisite for such bold action.

The success of this temporizing approach was not appreciated by all. Arran's contemporaries as well as many of the historians who have concerned themselves with his performance as governor failed to see the accomplishments

---

[1]Rev. James Moffat Scott, *The Martyrs of Angus and Mearns; Sketches in the History of the Scottish Reformation* (Paisley and London: Alexander Gardner, 1885), p. 123.

of his policy.

Various attributes of this policy manifested themselves in that the celebration of the peace coincided with the Scottish harvest and the removal of the young queen to Stirling--farther from Henry's grasping hands. Also, as the days of the campaign season for the English slipped by, the cause of Scottish nationalism, strengthened by a forthcoming renewal of "the auld alliance" with France, flowered. Although he was still far from joining forces with Beaton, Arran had already begun furthering the cause of Scottish nationalism by playing for time.

Following his ratification of the unpopular Greenwich treaties, Arran became convinced of his dwindling support within Scotland as well as his suspicion that Henry was soon going to have everything his own way in regard to the northern kingdom, treaties or otherwise. Hence, the governor gave his support in early September to the more obvious Scottish nationalists who championed "the auld alliance."

The main person through whom the English king hoped to fulfill his cherished dream of subverting Scottish sovereignty had slipped from his influence and had begun to wreck his once-thought ingenious diplomatic scheme. Unfortunately for Henry, he never fully realized that Arran could be such an ardent Scottish nationalist--nationalistic to the point of completely forsaking the security and promises of the pro-English party only to join ranks with his greatest domestic foe, Cardinal Beaton. As Andrew Lang, a nineteenth-century historian, maintained, Henry VIII was the giant in a fairy tale, always being deceived by little men.[2] The most important of these little men in

---

[2]Mackie, "Scotland," p. 114.

Scotland was the earl of Arran. The giant, however, would seek his revenge, still clinging to the Greenwich treaties long after the Scots had formally repudiated them and renewed the old accord with France.

Such revenge was regrettable, for both Henry VIII's and Protector Somerset's rough wooing brought them eventually a total repudiation of their cherished dream for a political union based upon a marriage between Edward and Mary. Repeated invasions merely convinced the nationalistic Arran that his faction-ridden kingdom's survival depended upon all the French support that it could get. Hence, England's loss was "the auld alliance's" gain. The French had a price for such needed support--the most important part of it being the cherished prize for all sides, the Hamiltons included--Mary Queen of Scots.

In consenting to the marriage of Mary to the young dauphin, the Scots convinced many an Englishman of the foolhardiness of their nation's rough wooing. By becoming a satellite of France, Scotland once again preserved her independence from England. For the Scots of the mid-sixteenth century inspired by a strong sense of national identity, there was very little less attractive than the rule of the English.

John Mackie, a historian of Anglo-Scottish relations, held that Protestantism, dislike of the French, common blood, as well as many other similar interests, worked towards a type of union between the two island kingdoms. Perhaps, if Henry and even Somerset had shown greater tact and restraint, both could have achieved more favorable results. Neither of the leaders, however, realized that if the fiercely independent Scots were ". . . to take up house with England," it would have to be "as a sister, not as a bondswoman."[3] The earl of Arran made a major contribution to this lack of perception and the failure of their political dream.

---

[3]Ibid.

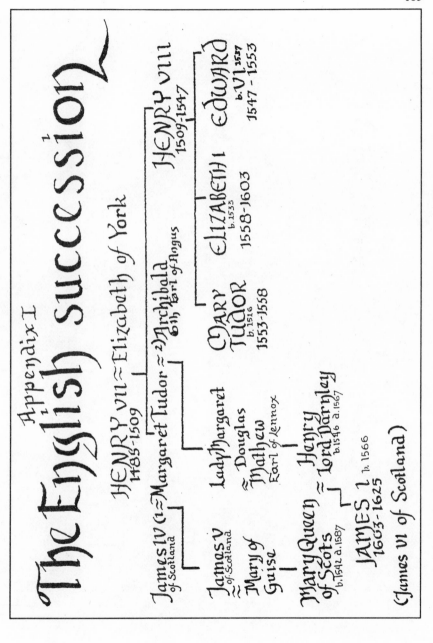

Appendix I

The English Succession

HENRY VII ≈ Elizabeth of York
1485–1509

HENRY VII ≈ Elizabeth of York
1485–1509

James IV (1≈ Margaret Tudor ≈ 2) Archibald   HENRY VIII
of Scotland   6th Earl of Angus   1509–1547

Lady Margaret   MARY   ELIZABETH I   EDWARD
≈ Douglas   TUDOR   b.1533   b.VI 1537
  Mathew   b.1516   1558–1603   1547–1553
  Earl of Lennox   1553–1558

James V
of Scotland

≈

Mary of
Guise

Mary Queen ≈ Henry
of Scots   Lord Darnley
b.1542 d.1587 b.1546 d.1567

JAMES I b.1566
1603–1625

(James VI of Scotland)

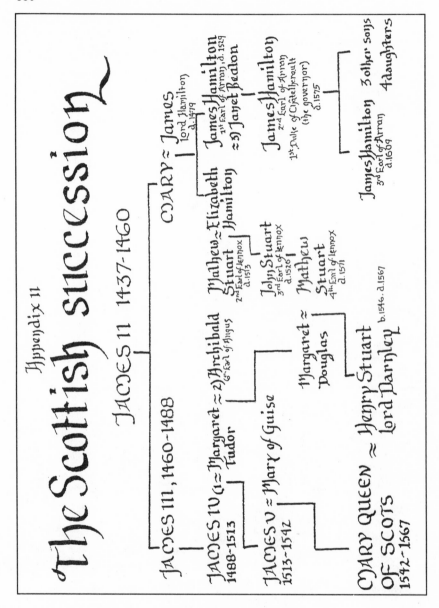

Appendix II

The Scottish succession

JAMES II 1437-1460

JAMES III, 1460-1488

JAMES IV (1= Margaret ≈ 2) Archibald
1488-1513   Tudor   6th Earl of Angus

JAMES V ≈ Mary of Guisa
1513-1542

                    Margaret ≈ Douglas

MARY QUEEN ≈ Henry Stuart
OF SCOTS   lord Darnley b.1546. d.1567
1542-1567

MARY ≈ James
        lord Hamilton
        d.1479

Mathew ≈ Elizabeth
Stuart   Hamilton
2nd Earl of lennox
d.1513

John Stuart
3rd Earl of lennox
d.1526

Mathew
Stuart
4th Earl of lennox
d.1571

James Hamilton
1st Earl of Arran, d.1529
≈ 5) Janet Beaton

James Hamilton
2nd Earl of Arran
1st Duke of Châtelherault
(the governor)
d.1575

James Hamilton   3 other sons
3rd Earl of Arran
d.1609   4 daughters

APPENDIX III

Henry VIII's Instructions to Sadler
25 April 1543.

Further, our pleasure is that if the governour be not tofarre swarved from us, befor tharryval of thise our lettres, youe shal eftsones repayr unto him and roundely, in a freendely sorte, saye unto him, 'Sir, what woll youe doo? Woll youe nowe wilfully cast yourself awaye? Can youe think otherwise but that the clergie knowing your opinions as they doo, woll seke all the wayes they can possible for your destruction, thoughe they give youe nowe fayr wordes to get their fate in the bushell? Or can youe think that youe shall contynue a governour when thadverse partie that wold have made themselves by a forged will regentes with youe, or rather excluded youe, shall have auctoritie, but youe shal soo be governed and compelled to doo their willes, as finally youe shal, whither youe woll or no, work your oune confusion? For Goddes sake, loke on it in tyme, and considre what honour youe and your posteritie may be sure of at the kinges majeste my maisters hande, if youe applie to him and yeve not thother partie cause soo to note youe inconstant, as they shal feare a like turn when they have youe inconstant, as they shal feare a like turn when they have youe, and the rather for the same divise howe shortly and spedily to end youe. This I saye to youe for the discharge of my dieuty to the kinges majeste, who lovethe youe and wold your honour and proffit, and youe may be wel assured hathe caused nothing to be said or writen to youe but for a declaration of his zeale in thadvauncement of the same, and for no feare or regarde that youe shal in any wise hindre his majestes most godly purpose, thoughe youe wold wilfully in the meane season hazarde yourself and your state for ever, which I pray God youe may considre as youe have cause.'[1]

---

[1]From *Hamilton Papers*, 1:527-8, Henry 8 to Sadler, 25 April 1543.

SELECTED BIBLIOGRAPHY

Manuscripts

The following manuscript collections are all found in the British Library in London.

Additional - 10,012, 23,108, 32,091, 32,649, 32,650, 32,651, 32,652, 32,653, and 33,531.

Cotton, Caligula B IV and VIII.

Egerton - 1818

Royal - 18 B VI

Sloane - 3199

Printed Sources

A Source Book of Scottish History, 1424 to 1567. Edited by William C. Dickinson, Gordon Donaldson, and Isabel Milne. 3 vols, Edinburgh: Thomas Nelson and Sons, Ltd., 1952-1954.

Brown, Peter H., editor. *Scotland Before 1700 from Contemporary Documents.* Edinburgh: David Douglas, 1893.

Buchanan, George. *The History of Scotland from the Earliest Accounts of that Nation, to the Reign of King James VI.* Edited by Mr. Bond. 2 vols. London: S. Palmer, 1722.

Byrne, M. St. Clare, editor. *The Letters of King Henry VIII: A Selection, with a few other Documents*. London: Cassell and Co. Ltd., 1968.

Cameron, Annie Isabella, editor. *The Scottish Correspondence of Mary of Lorraine: Including Some Three Hundred Letters from 20th February 1542-1543 to 15th May 1560*. Scottish History Society Publications, third series, vol. 10. Edinburgh: University Press, 1927.

_____. *The Warrender Papers*. 2 vols. Scottish History Society Publications, third series, vols. 18 and 19. Edinburgh: University Press, 1931.

Clifford, Arthur, editor. *The State Papers and Letters of Sir Ralph Sadler, Knight-Banneret: To Which Is Added a Memoir of the Life of Sir Ralph Sadler, with Historical Notes by Walter Scott, Esq.* 2 vols. Edinburgh: Archibald Constable and Co., 1809.

Dickinson, Gladys, editor. *Two Missions of Jacques de la Brosse: An Account of the Affairs of Scotland in the Year 1543 and the Journal of the Siege of Leith, 1560*. Scottish Historical Society Publications, third series, vol. 36. Edinburgh: University Press, 1942.

Ellis, Henry, editor. *Original Letters, Illustrative of English History; Including Numerous Royal Letters: From Autographs in the British Museum, and One or Two Other Collections. With Notes and Illustrations.* First series, 3 vols. second edition. London: Harding, Triphook, and Lepard, 1825. Second series, 4 vols. London: Harding and Lepard, 1827. Third series, 4 vols. London: Richard Bentley, 1846.

English Historical Documents, 1485-1558. Edited by Charles H. Williams. London: Eyre and Spottiswoode. 1967.

Facsimiles of National Manuscripts of Scotland. Edited by Sir William Gibson. Edinburgh: Her Majesty's General Register House, 1872.

Foedera, Conventiones, Literae, et Cujuscunque Generis Acta Publica, Inter Reges Angliae, et Alios Quosvis Imperatores, Reges, Pontifices, Principes, Vel Communitates, ab Ineunte Saeculo Duodecimo, viz. ab Anno 1101, ad nostra usque Tempors, Habita aut Tractata; Ex Autographis, infra Secretiores Archivorum Regiorum Thesaurarias, Per

Multa Saecula Reconditis, Fideliter Escripta. Edited by Thomas Rymer. 2nd ed. 20 vols. London: J. Tonson, 1726-1735.

Great Britain, General Registry Office of Births, Deaths, and Marriages. *The Hamilton Papers: Letters and Papers Illustrating the Political Relations of England and Scotland in the XVIth Century, Formerly in the Possession of the Dukes of Hamilton, Now in the British Museum.* Edited by Joseph Bain. 2 vols. Edinburgh: Her Majesty's General Register House, 1890.

Great Britain. *Historical Manuscripts Commission, Calendar of the Manuscripts of the Most Hon. Marquis of Salisbury, K. G., etc., etc., etc. Preserved at Hartfield House, Hertfordshire.* 11 vols. London: Her Majesty's Stationery Office, 1883-1906.

_____. *Historical Manuscripts Commission, Eleventh Report, Appendix, Part VI. The Manuscripts of the Duke of Hamilton, K.T.* London: Her Majesty's Stationery Office, 1887.

_____. *Historical Manuscripts Commission, Fifth Report of the Royal Commission on Historical Manuscripts, Part I, Report and Appendix.* London: Her Majesty's Stationary Office, 1876.

_____. *Historical Manuscripts Commission, Twelfth Report, Appendix, Part IV. The Manuscripts of His Grace the Duke of Rutland, G.C.B., Preserved at Belvoir Castle.* London: Her Majesty's Stationery Office, 1888.

Great Britain. Public Record Office. *Acts of the Lords of Council in Public Affairs 1501-1554. Selections from the Acts Dominorum Concilii Introductory to the Register of the Privy Council of Scotland.* Edited by Robert Kerr Hannay. Edinburgh: His Majesty's General Register House. 1932.

_____. *Acts of the Privy Council of England.* Edited by John Darent et al. 46 vols., new series. London: Her Majesty's Stationery Office, 1890-1964.

_____. *Calendar of Letters, Despatches and State Papers Relating to Negotiations between England and Spain Preserved in the Archives at Simancas and Elsewhere.* Edited by Royall Tyler et al. 13 vols. London:

Her Majesty's Stationery Office, 1862-1954.

_____. *Calendar of State Papers and Manuscripts Relating to English Affairs, Existing in the Archives and Collections of Venice, and Other Libraries of Northern Italy.* Edited by Rawdon Brown et al. 38 vols. London: Longmans, Green, Reader, and Dyer, 1864- .

_____. *Calendar of State Papers, Domestic Series of the Reigns of Edward VI, Mary, Elizabeth 1547-1580, Preserved in the State Paper Department of Her Majesty's Public Record Office.* Edited by Robert Lemon. London: Longman, Brown, Green, Longmans, and Roberts 1859.

_____. *Calendar of State Papers, Foreign Series, of the Reign of Edward VI, 1547-1553, Preserved in the State Paper Department of Her Majesty's Public Record Office.* Edited by Donald Turnbull. London: Longman, Green, Longman, and Roberts, 1861.

_____. *Calendar of State Papers Relating to Scotland and Mary, Queen of Scots 1547-1603. Preserved in the Public Record Office, the British Museum and Elsewhere in England.* Edited by Joseph Bain et al. 13 vols. Edinburgh: Her Majesty's General Register House, 1898-1969.

_____. *Calendar of State Papers Relating to Scotland Preserved in the State Paper Department of Her Majesty's Public Record Office; the Scottish Series of the Reigns of Henry VIII, Edward VI, Mary, Elizabeth, 1509-1589.* Edited by Markham J. Thorpe. 2 vols. London: Longman, Brown, Green, Longmans, and Roberts, 1858.

_____. *Compota Thesaurariorum Regum Scotorum. Accounts of the Lord High Treasurer of Scotland.* Edited by Thomas Dickson and James Balfour Paul. 11 vols. Edinburgh: Her Majesty's Stationery Office, 1877-1916.

_____. *Letters and Papers, Foreign and Domestic, of the Reign of Henry VIII, 1509-1547. Preserved in the Public Record Office, the British Museum, and Elsewhere in England.* Edited by James Gairdner and Robert H. Brodie, et al. 21 vols. in 33. London: Her Majesty's Stationery Office, 1862-1932.

_____. *Registrum Magni Sigilli Regum Scotorum. The Register of the Great Seal of Scotland.* Edited by James B. Paul and John M. Thomason. 11 vols. Edinburgh: Her Majesty's General Register House, 1882-1914.

_____. *Registrum secreti sigilli regum Scotorum: the Register of the Privy Seal of Scotland.* Edited by James Beveridge. 7 vols. Edinburgh: His Majesty's Stationery Office, 1908-1965.

_____. *Rotuli Scaccarii Regum Scotorum. The Exchequer Rolls of Scotland.* Edited by George Powell MacNeill et al. 23 vols. Edinburgh: Her Majesty's General Register House, 1878-1908.

_____. *The Acts of the Parliaments of Scotland.* Collected by Thomas Thomson and Cosmo Innes. 12 vols. London: His Majesty's Stationery Office, 1814-1875.

_____. *The Letters of James V.* Collected and calendared by Robert Kerr Hannay. Edited by Denys Hay. Edinburgh: Her Majesty's Stationery Office, 1954.

_____. *The Register of the Privy Council of Scotland.* Edited by John Hill Burton and Donald Masson. 14 vols., first series. Edinburgh: Her Majesty's General Register House, 1877-1898.

_____. *The Statutes of the Realm. Printed by Command of His Majesty King George the Third in Pursuance of An Address of the House of Commons of Great Britain. From Original Records and Authentic Manuscripts.* Edited by A. Luders et al. 11 vols. London: His Majesty's Stationery Office, 1810-1828.

Great Britain. Record Commission. *State Papers Published under the Authority of His Majesty's Commission: Henry VIII.* 11 vols. London: His Majesty's Commission, 1830-1852.

Haynes, Samuel, editor. *A Collection of State Papers Relating to Affairs In the Reigns of King Henry VIII, King Edward VI, Queen Mary, and Queen Elizabeth, From the Year 1542-1570. Transcribed from Original Letters and Other Authentick Memorials, Never Before Publish'd, Left by William Cecill Lord Burghley, and Now Remaining at Hatfield House, in the Library of the Right Honourable the Present Earl of Salisbury.* London: William Bowyer. 1740.

Knox, John. *History of the Reformation in Scotland.* First published 1584. Edited by William Croft Dickinson. 2 vols. London: Thomas Nelson and Sons, 1949.

Lindsay, Robert of Pitscottie. *The Historie and Chronicles of Scotland From the Slauchter of King James the First to the Ane Thousande Fyve Hundreith Thrie Scoir Fyftein Zeit, Written and Collected by Robert Lindesay of Pitscottie Being a Continuation of the Translation of the Chronicles Written by Hector Boece, and Translated by John Bellenden. Now First Published from Two of the Oldest Manuscripts, One Bequeathed by Dr. David Laing to the University of Edinburgh, and the Other in the Library of John Scott of Halkshill.* Edited by Aeneas James George Mackay. 3 vols. Edinburgh: William Blackwood and Sons, 1899. Printed for the Scottish Text Society.

Lodge, Edmund, editor. *Illustrations of British History, Biography, and Manners, in the Reigns of Henry VIII, Edward VI, Mary, Elizabeth, and James I, Exhibited in a Series of Original Papers, Selected from the Manuscripts of the Noble Families of Howard, Talbot, and Cecil; Containing, Among a Variety of Interesting Pieces, A Great Part of the Correspondence of Elizabeth, and Her Ministers, With George, the Sixth Earl of Shrewsbury, During the Fifteen Years in Which Mary Queen of Scots Remained in His Custody: With Numerous Notes and Observations.* 3 vols. London: G. Nicol, 1791.

Maitland Club. *Selections from Unpublished Manuscripts in the College of Arms and the British Museum Illustrating the Reign of Mary Queen of Scotland.* Edited by Joseph Stevenson. Glasgow: The Maitland Club, 1837.

Maxwell, John - 4th Baron Lord Herris. *Historical Memoirs of the Reign of Mary Queen of Scots, and a Portion of the Reign of King James the Sixth.* Edinburgh: n.p., 1836.

Melville, Sir James. *Memoirs of Sir James Melville of Halhill, 1535-1617.* Edited with an Introduction by A. Francis Stewart. London: George

Routledge and Sons, Ltd., 1929.

Miscellany of the Scottish History Society (Second Volume). Scottish History Society Publications, first series, vol. 44. Edinburgh: University Press, 1904.

Nichols, John Gough, editor. *Literary Remains of Edward VI*. 2 vols. London: Roxburghe Club, 1857.

Patten, William. *The Expedition into Scotland of the Most Worthy Fortunate Prince Edward, Duke of Somerset, Uncle unto Our Most Noble Sovereign Lord and King's Majesty Edward the VI. Governor of His Highness' Person, and Protector of His Grace's Realmes, Dominions and Subjects: Made in the First Year of His Majesty's Most Prosperous Reign, and Set Out by Way of Diary, by W. Patten Londoner.* n.p., 1548; reprint ed., New York: Da Capo Press Inc., 1972.

Selve, Odet de. *Correspondence politique 1546-1549*. Edited by G. Lefevre-Pontalis. Paris: 1888.

Spotswood, John. *The History of the Church of Scotland, Beginning the Year of our Lord 203, and Continued to the End of the Reign of King James the VI. of Ever Blessed Memory. Wherein are Described, the Progress of Christianity: the Persecutions and Interruptions of It; the Foundations of Churches; the Erecting of Bishopricks; the Building and Endowing of Monasteries, and Other Religious Places; the Succession of Bishops in Their Sees; the Reformation of Religion, and the Frequent Disturbances of That Nation by Wars, Conspiracies, Tumults, Schisms. Together With Great Variety of Other Matters, Both Ecclesiasticall and Politicall.* London: F. Flesher, 1655.

Teulet, Alexandre, editor. *Relations Politiques dé la France et de l'Éspangne avec l'Éscosse au XVIc Siècle, Papiers d'État, Pièces et Documents Inédits ou Peu Connus Tirés Des Bibliothèques et des Archives de France.* 5 vols. Paris: Veuve Jules Renouard, 1862.

The Complaynt of Scotlande: ane Exortatione to the Thre Estaits to be vigilante in the Deffens of their Public veil. 1549. With an appendix of Contemporary English Tracts; The Just Declaration of Henry VIII

(1542); The Exhortacion of James Harrysone, Scottishmen (1547); The Epistle of the Lord Protector Somerset (1548); The Epitome of Nicholas Bodrugan alias Adams (1548). Reedited from the originals with Introduction and Glossary by James A. H. Murray. London: N. Trubner and Co., 1872.

Thomson, Thomas, editor. *A Diurnal of Remarkable Occurrents that Have Passed Within the Country of Scotland Since the Death of King James the Fourth till the Year M.D. LXXV.* Edinburgh: The Bannatyne Club, 1833.

Tudor Royal Proclamations, 1485-1603. Edited by Paul L. Hughes and James F. Larkin. 3 vols. New Haven: Yale University Press, 1964-1969.

Tudor Tracts, 1532-1588. Introduction by A. F. Pollard. New York: E. P. Dutton and Co., n.d.

Wood, Marguerite, editor. *Foreign Correspondence with Marie de Lorraine, Queen of Scotland, from the Originals in the Balcarres Papers, 1537-1557.* Scottish Historical Society Publications, third series, vols. 4 and 7. Edinburgh: University Press, 1923-1925.

Secondary Works

Anderson, William. *The Scottish Nation: or the Surnames, Families, Literature, Honours and Biographical History of the People of Scotland.* 3 vols. Edinburgh: A. Fullarton and Co., 1863.

Beer, Barrett L. *Northumberland: The Political Career of John Dudley, Earl of Warwick and Duke of Northumberland.* n.p.: Kent State University Press, 1973.

Bindoff, S. T. *Tudor England.* Baltimore: Penguin Books Inc., 1950.

Bingham, Caroline. *James V, King of Scots, 1512-1542.* London: Collins, 1971.

_____. *The Stewart Kingdom of Scotland, 1371-1603.* London: Weidenfeld and Nicolson, 1974.

Brown, Peter Hume. *History of Scotland.* 3 vols. Cambridge: Cambridge University Press, 1912.

Burton, John Hill. *The History of Scotland, From Agricola's Invasion to the Extinction of the Last Jacobite Insurrection.* 8 vols. Edinburgh: William Blackwood and Son, 1873.

Bush, M. L. *The Government Policy of Protector Somerset.* Montreal: McGill-Queen's University Press, 1975.

Chapman, Hester W. *The Last Tudor king: A Study of Edward VI.* New York: Macmillan, 1959.

Cowan, Ian. *The Scottish Reformation: Church and Society in Sixteenth-Century Scotland.* New York: St. Martin's Press, 1982.

Dickinson, William Croft. *Scotland from the Earliest Times to 1603.* London and Edinburgh: Thomas Nelson and Sons, Ltd., 1961.

Dictionary of National Biography from the Earliest Times to 1900. Edited by Leslie Stephen and Sidney Lee. 22 vols. 2nd ed. London: Oxford University Press, 1949-50.

Donaldson, Gordon. *All the Queen's Men: Power and Politics in Mary Stewart's Scotland.* New York: St. Martin's Press, 1983.

_____. *The Auld Alliance.* Published by the Saltire Society. New York: State Mutual Book and Periodical Service Ltd. 1986.

_____. *Scotland: James V to James VII.* The Edinburgh History of Scotland series, vol. 3. Edinburgh and London: Oliver and Boyd, 1965.

_____. *Scottish Church History.* Edinburgh: Scottish Academic Press, 1985.

Drummond, Humphrey. *Our Man in Scotland: Sir Robert Sadleir, 1507-1587.* London: Leslie Frewin, 1969.

198

Eaves, Richard Glen. *Henry VIII and James V's Regency 1524-1528: A Study in Anglo-Scottish Diplomacy*. Lanham, Maryland: University Press of America, 1987.

_____. *Henry VIII's Scottish Diplomacy, 1513-1524; England's Relations with the Regency of James V*. New York: Exposition Press, 1971.

Elton, Geoffrey R. *Henry VIII: An Essay in Revision*. London: Routledge and Kegan Paul, 1962.

_____. *Reform and Reformation: England 1509-1558*. Cambridge, Massachusetts: Harvard University Press, 1977.

_____. *The Tudor Revolution in Government: Adminstrative Changes in the Reign of Henry VIII*. Cambridge: Cambridge University Press, 1953.

Erickson, Carolly. *Great Harry: The Extravagant Life of Henry VIII*. New York: Summit Books, 1980.

Ferguson, William. *Scotland's Relations with England: A Survey to 1707*. Edinburgh: John Donald Publishers Ltd., 1977.

Fisher, Herbert Albert Laurens. *The History of England from the Accession of Henry VII to the Death of Henry VIII, 1485-1547*. New York: Longmans, Green, and Co., 1906.

Fleming, David Hay. *Mary Queen of Scots from Her Birth to Her Flight into England: A Brief Biography: With Critical Notes, a Few Documents Hitherto Unpublished, and an Itinerary*. London: Hodder and Stoughton, 1898.

Forneron, Henri. *Les Ducs de Guise et Leur Époque; Étude Historique sur le Seizième Siècle*. Paris: E. Plon, 1877.

Fraser, Antonia. *Mary Queen of Scots*. New York: Delacorte Press, 1969.

_____. *The Wives of Henry VIII*. New York: Vintage Books, 1994.

Froude, James Anthony. *History of England from the Fall of Wolsey to the*

Death of Elizabeth. 12 vols. New York: Charles Scribner, 1872.

Goodman, Anthony. *A History of England from Edward II ot James I.* London and New York: Longman, 1977.

Grant, Alexander. *Independence and Nationhood: Scotland 1306-1469.* Edinburgh: Edinburgh University Press, 1991.

Grimm, Harold J. *The Reformation Era, 1500-1650.* 2nd ed. New York: The Macmillan Company, 1973.

Gunn, Steven J. *Charles Brandon, Duke of Suffolk c 1484-1545.* Oxford: Blackwell, 1988.

Hamilton, George. *A History of the House of Hamilton.* Edinburgh: J. Skinner and Co., Ltd., 1933.

Hannay, Robert Kerr and Herkless, John. *The Archbishops of St. Andrews.* Vol. 4: *David Beaton.* Edinburgh and London: W. Blackwood and Sons, 1913.

Henderson, T. F. *Mary Queen of Scots: Her Environment and Tragedy: A Biography.* 2 vols. London: Hutchinson and Co., 1905.

Hoskins, W. G. *The Age of Plunder: King Henry's England, 1500-1547.* London and New York: Longman, 1976.

Houston, R. A. and Whyte, I. D., editors. *Scottish Society, 1500-1800.* Cambridge: Cambridge University Press, 1989.

Jordan, W. K. *Edward VI the Young King: The Protectorship of the Duke of Somerset.* Cambridge, Massachusetts: Harvard University Press, 1968.

_____. *Edward VI: The Threshold of Power: The Dominance of the Duke of Northumberland.* Cambridge, Massachusetts: Harvard University Press, 1970.

Keith, Robert. *The History of the Affairs of Church and State in Scotland, from the Beginning of the Reformation in the Reign of King James V to the*

Retreat of Queen Mary into England, Anno 1568. Taken from the Publick Records and Other Authentick Vouchers. 3 vols. Edinburgh: Printed by Thomas and Walter Ruddimans for George Stewart and Alexander Symmer, 1734.

La Brosse, Jules de. *Histoire d'un Capitaine Bourbonnais au XVIe Siècle. Jacques de La Brosse, 1485 (?)--1562. Ses Missions en Écosse.* Paris: Librairie Ancienne Honoré Champion, 1929.

Lang, Andrew. *John Knox and the Reformation.* London: Longmans, Green, and Co., 1905.

Lodge, Edmund. *Life of Cardinal Béthune.* London: 1821.

MacDougall N., editor. *Church, Politics and Society: Scotland 1408-1929.* Edinburgh: John Donald Publishers Ltd., 1983.

Mackie, John D. "Henry VIII and Scotland." *Transactions of the Royal Historical Society.* Fourth series, no. 29. London: Offices of the Royal Historical Society, 1947.

_____. *The Earlier Tudors, 1485-1558.* The Oxford History of England Series, vol. 7. Oxford: Clarendon Press, 1952.

Mackie, R. L. *King James IV of Scotland: A Brief Survey of His Life and Times.* Edinburgh and London: Oliver and Boyd, 1958.

Marshall, Rosalind Kay. *Mary of Guise.* London: Collins, 1977.

Mason, Roger, editor. *Scotland and England 1286-1815.* Edinburgh: John Donald Publishers Ltd., 1987.

Mattingly, Garrett. *Renaissance Diplomacy.* London: Jonathan Cape, 1955.

Michel, Francisque. *Les Écossais en France, Les Français en Écosse.* 2 vols. London: Trubner and Co., 1862.

Mignet, Francis Auguste Marie Alexis. *The History of Mary Queen of Scots.* Translated by A. R. Scoble. 2 vols. London: Richard Bentley, 1851.

Mitchison, Rosalind. *A History of Scotland*. London: Methuen and Co., Ltd., 1970.

Oman, Sir Charles. *A History of the Art of War in the Sixteenth Century*. London: Methuen and Co., Ltd., 1937.

Pollard, Albert F. *England Under Protector Somerset*. London: K. Paul, Trench, Trubner and Co., 1900.

_____. *Henry VIII*. London: Logmans, Green, 1951.

Rae, Thomas I. *The Administration of the Scottish Frontier, 1513-1603*. Edinburgh: University Press, 1966.

Read, Conyers. *The Tudors: Personalities and Practical Politics in Sixteenth Century England*. Oxford: Clarendon Press, 1953.

Ridley, Jasper. *Henry VIII: The Politics of Tyranny*. New York: Fromm International, 1986.

_____. *John Knox*. New York and Oxford: Oxford University Press, 1968.

Ridpath, George. *The Border - History of England and Scotland, Deduced from the Earliest times to the Union of the Two Crowns: Comprehending A Particular Detail of the Transactions of the Two Nations with One Another: Accounts of Remarkable Antiquities; and A Variety of Interesting Anecdotes of the Most Considerable Families and Distinguished Characters in Both Kingdoms*. Revised by Philip Ridpath. London: T. Cadell et al., 1776.

Sanderson, Margaret. *Cardinal of Scotland, David Beaton, c 1494-1546*. Edinburgh: John Donald Publishers Ltd., 1986.

Scarisbrick, John J. *Henry VIII*. Berkeley and Los Angeles: University of California Press, 1968.

Scott, Rev. James Moffat. *The Martyrs of Angus and Mearns: Sketches in the History of the Scottish Reformation*. Paisley and London: Alexander Gardner, 1885.

Slavin, A. J. *Politics and Profit: A Study of Sir Ralph Sadler, 1507-1547.* Cambridge: Cambridge University Press, 1966.

Smith, Lacey Baldwin. *Henry VIII: The Mask of Royalty.* Boston: Houghton Mifflin Co., 1971.

Smith, Preserved. *The Age of the Reformation.* New York: Henry Holt and Co., 1920.

Squair, Olive M. *Scotland in Europe: A Study in Race Relations.* 2nd ed. Inverness: Graphic Publications, 1977.

Taylor, James. *The Great Historic Families of Scotland.* 2 vols. London: J. S. Virtue and Co., Ltd., 1890.

Tytler, Patrick F. *The History of Scotland, from the Accession of Alexander III to the Union.* 9 vols. Edinburgh: William Tait Publishers, 1828-1843.

Weber, Bernerd Clarke. "Personalities and Politics at the Court of Henry II of France, 1547-1559." *Studies in Modern European History in Honor of Franklin Charles Palm.* New York: Bookman Associates, Inc. 1956.

_____. *The Youth of Mary Queen of Scots.* Philadelphia: Dorrance and Co., 1941.

Weir, Alison. *The Six Wives of Henry VIII.* New York: Ballantine Books, 1993.

Weisse, Jane Lee (Hunt). *A History of the Bethune Family. Translated from the Frence of Andre du Chesne, with Additions from Family Records and Other Available Sources.* By Mrs. John A. Weisse. New York: Trow's Printing and Bookbinding Co., 1884.

Wormald, Jenny. *Court, Kirk, and Community: Scotland 1470-1625.* Edinburgh: Edinburgh University Press, 1991.

Articles

Anderson, Rev. William J. "Rome and Scotland, 1513-1625." *The Innes Review* 10 (1959): 173-93.

Barrow, Geoffrey. "The Anglo-Scottish Border." *Northern History* 1 (1966): 21-42.

Brown, Peter Hume. "The Scottish Nobility and Their Part in the National History." *Scottish Historical Review* 3 (1906): 157-170.

Bryce, W. M. "Mary Stuart's Voyage to France in 1548." *English Historical Review* 22 (January 1907): 43-50.

Burns, J. H. "The Political Background of the Reformation, 1513-1625." *The Innes Review* 10 (1959): 199-234.

Clark, J.C.D. "English History's Forgotten Context: Scotland, Ireland, Wales." *Historical Journal* 32 (1989): 211-28.

Cowan, Ian. "Anglo-Scottish Relations." *Historical Journal* 32 (1989): 229-35.

Dickinson, Gladys. "Instructions to the French Ambassador, 30 March 1550." *Scottish Historical Review* 26 (1947): 154-167.

_____. "Some Notes on the Scottish Army in the First Half of the Sixteenth Century." *Scottish Historical Review* 28 (1949): 133-45.

Fisher, A. "A Patriot for Whom? Wallace and Bruce: Scotland's Unearly Heroes." *History Today* 39 (1989): 18-23.

Hannay, R. K.; Harvey, Jane; and Wood, Marguerite. "Some Papal Bulls among the Hamilton Papers." *Scottish Historical Review* 22 (1924): 25-41.

Hannay, R. K. "Letters of the Papal Legate in Scotland, 1543." *Scottish Historical Review* 11 (1913):1-26.

_____. "The Earl of Arran and Queen Mary." *Scottish Historical Review* 18 (1921): 258-76.

Head, David M. "Henry VIII's Scottish Policy: A Reassessment." *Scottish Historical Review* 61 (1982): 1-24.

Healey, R. M. "John Knox's *History*; A 'Compleat' Sermon in Christian Duty." *Church History* 61 (1992): 319-33.

Lang, Andrew. "The Cardinal and the King's Will." *Scottish Historical Review* 3 (1906): 410-22.

MacDougall, N. "The Kingship of James IV of Scotland: The Glory of All Princely Governing?" *History Today* 34 (1984): 30-6.

Mackenzie, William. "The Debateable Land." *Scottish Historical Review* 30 (1951): 109-25.

Mahoney, Matthew. "The Scottish Hierarchy, 1513-1565." *The Innes Review* 10 (1959): 21-66.

McEwen, J. "Battle of Floddon." *History Today* 8 (1958): 337-45.

McKean, C. "Hamilton of Finnart." *History Today* 43 (1993): 42-7.

Merriman, M. H. "The Assured Scots: Scottish Collaborators with England during the Rough Wooing." *Scottish Historical Review* 47 (1968): 10-34.

Weber, Bernerd Clarke, and Van Scoy, Herbert. "The Marriage of Mary Queen of Scots and the Dauphin." *Scottish Historical Review* 31 (1952): 41-48.

Wormald, Jenny. "Bloodfeud, Kindred, and Government in Early Modern Scotland." *Past and Present* 87 (1980): 54-97.

_____. "The House of Stewart and Its Realm." *History Today* 34 (1984): 21-7.

_____, "Scottish Disputes." *History Today* 35 (1985): 59-60.

INDEX

STUDIES IN BRITISH HISTORY